D1551314

PUBLISHER'S NOTE: Much of the material in this book first appeared in a large-format pictorial volume (now out of print) titled *Fort Bliss: An Illustrated History* (Mangan Books, 1981). This revised version is updated and contains a new introduction by Leon C. Metz.

Desert Army

Leon C. Mott

BOOKS BY LEON C. METZ

John Selman: Gunfighter

Dallas Stoudenmire: El Paso Marshal

Pat Garrett: Story of a Western Lawman

The Shooters

City at the Pass

Fort Bliss: An Illustrated History

Turning Points of El Paso, Texas

Desert Army: Fort Bliss on the Texas Border

Border: The U.S.-Mexico Line

Southern New Mexico Empire

Roadside History of Texas

El Paso Chronicles

Desert Army

Fort Bliss on the Texas Border

by Leon C. Metz

MANGAN BOOKS
El Paso, Texas

To Jimmy

who joined the Navy

Introduction

THE CONCEPT FOR THIS BOOK began at the Cattleman's Steakhouse at Indian Cliffs Ranch in Fabens, Texas, when publishers Frank and Judy Mangan met with my wife Cheryl and me for dinner. Over steaks and margaritas, we discussed past and present projects, finally noting that a full history of Fort Bliss had never been written or published.

Frank wanted a pictorial book; I argued for a more definitive history. Neither convinced the other, and we left it at that. Two hours later, Frank called at midnight, proposing a deal. He would make his pictorial book thicker, if I would make my voluminous history smaller. Commander (Ret.) Millard McKinney, the southwestern authority on historical Fort Bliss, would provide photos and expertise.

An agreement was reached. Mangan Books published *Fort Bliss: An Illustrated History* in 1981.

The book won all sorts of awards. It never had an unfavorable evaluation, and was reviewed all over the country. The military post used it as a gift for visiting dignitaries.

Still, when the first edition sold out, the book's high cost in its original format did not justify another printing. Yet, the book served a purpose. This was the only Fort Bliss history in existence. It described the relationship between a town and a military facility. It outlined Spanish and Mexican military roots prior to Fort Bliss. Precise maps pinpointed the five previous Fort Bliss sites. A heavy emphasis explained Pancho Villa and the Mexican Revolution, factors largely responsible for the present size and greatness of Fort Bliss. Finally, there were chapters on William Beaumont Army Medical Center, White Sands Missile Range and Biggs Air Force Base.

In this revised, updated edition, the basic story remains. It is the history of a desert army at the Pass of the North, of a mighty post that expanded from a few, scattered adobe buildings at frontier El Paso to become a world-wide defender of liberty.

— Leon C. Metz

Contents

Early seventeenth century Spanish nobleman at Paso del Norte. (Jose Cisneros)

The Europeans 1

FORT BLISS IS one of the oldest, largest, and most important military bases in the United States. The complex which it represents (including White Sands Missile Range) is one reason why Americans sleep well at night. For a century and a half, Fort Bliss has trained infantrymen, cavalrymen, artillerymen and missilemen from dozens of countries and from all fifty states. Yet its history has never been told in any detail, its song has never been sung.

It would not be altogether correct to call Fort Bliss the free world's foremost military bastion, but without Fort Bliss the free world would be in serious danger, and perhaps could not survive.

It would also not be correct to call Fort Bliss the only economic breadbasket for the El Paso Southwest. But without the $500 million pumped annually into the city's economy, the growth of El Paso and its surrounding communities would certainly slide into serious decline.

Fort Bliss guards the Pass of the North, where three states (Texas, New Mexico and Chihuahua), and two nations (the United States and Mexico) meet. Here is the gateway south into Mexico and north into the United States.

For over a century the military post at Fort Bliss has kept the peace and bolstered the local economy. Yet Fort Bliss was not the initial military presence. When Major Jefferson Van Horne in 1849 marched his 3rd Infantry into El Paso, the area already had a splendid military heritage. There had been combatants here before.

Early man risked his life against the mastodon, the mammoth and the fierce dire wolf during the thousands of years when a huge savanna comprised what is today Fort Bliss. As the centuries moved along, the region gradually assumed the properties of a desert. That is how the Europeans found it four hundred years ago. Near what is now El Paso, the Spaniards encountered the Suma Indians, eaters of the mesquite bean and the prickly pear, and the Manso Indians, who consumed raw fish. The Rodríguez-Chamuscado Expedition entered the Pass on June 5, 1581, the Spaniards having twin hopes: to Christianize the Indians and to find mineral wealth. Nine soldiers and three priests, plus servants and livestock, intrepidly followed the Conchos River from Santa Bárbara, Chihuahua to its junction with the Rio Grande. Then they turned northwest along the latter stream.

The expedition entered New Mexico where one priest decided to return home, and was murdered by Indians within a few miles. The remaining two padres took it upon themselves, against military advice, to stay and preach the gospel. After the soldiers left, the friars also were slain, their exact fate remaining a mystery for years.

A relief effort led by Captain Antonio de Espejo, composed of fourteen soldiers, reached the Pass one year later on its way north. With Espejo there is little to commend as he was both a scoundrel and accused murderer. Most historians suspect he sought information about the priests in order to redeem himself with the Church and Crown. We remember Espejo partly because he named New Mexico.

The first substantial military recognition belongs to Juan de Oñate, although he was actually more of a colonist than a conquistador. He brought approximately 400 men, 183 families, 83 wagons and thousands of sheep, horses, cattle, goats and mules to the Pass. After reaching the Rio Grande on April 20, 1598, in the present vicinity of San Elizario, Texas (twenty miles southeast of downtown El Paso), Oñate took possession in the name of King Philip of Spain. A week later he forded the Rio Grande where El Paso is today. Before entering New Mexico, he named the crossing, *El Paso del Río del Norte* (the Crossing of the River to the North).

Over half a century went by before Catholic missionaries settled at the Pass. By 1659, they had erected a cornerstone of the *Misión Nuestra Señora de Guadalupe* (Our Lady of Guadalupe Mission). Paso del Norte, later named Ciudad Juárez, dates from that time.

When the Pueblo Indians revolted against Spanish oppression in northern New Mexico during 1680, Spanish refugees fled the burning countryside around Santa Fe and sought safety in Paso del Norte. Convinced that a quick reentry was impossible, Governor Antonio Otermín ordered permanent villages established for the loyal Indians. One was Ysleta (named for Isleta, near Albuquerque) which housed the Tigua Indians, and another was Socorro (for Socorro, New Mexico), which contained the Piros. Ysleta is presently incorporated into El Paso, and Socorro is in El Paso's legal jurisdiction.

Spain did not reconquer Santa Fe until 1693. Meanwhile its abandoned Spanish horses formed the nucleus of wild mustang herds. Comanches swiftly became superior horsemen, and promptly drove the Apaches from the southern plains, sending them retreating westward toward the Rio Grande and New Mexico. There they encountered the Spanish, an adversary upon which to vent their frustration.

For essentially the first time in its New World history, Spain faced a mobile enemy. The horse had changed the art of warfare.

To meet the challenge, Spain ordered the Marqués de Rubí, a respected military leader, to reorganize frontier defenses. Rubí proposed a cordon of fifteen presidios (forts) strung from gulf to gulf across the rim of empire.

Many of Rubí's recommendations were implemented in the Royal Regulations of 1772, and Colonel Hugo O'Conor, an Irish mercenary, was commissioned as commandant-inspector to place them into effect.

Altogether O'Conor built or relocated twelve presidios. In early 1774, he transferred the presidio of Guajoquilla from southern Chihuahua to the Valley of San Elizario, fifty-four miles downstream from Paso del Norte. In February, 1780, as the Americans were winding down their Revolutionary War, the Presidio of San Elizario was ordered to its present location, now five miles outside the city limits of El Paso, Texas.

San Elizario was of rectangular shape, whereas most presidios were square. The adobe defense walls

Presidio soldiers held the line against Apaches and other marauding Indians, yet are little known today. They were uneducated, abused by country and officers, but good fighters and durable, tough militia. They enabled the Spanish to survive. (Jose Cisneros)

were about ten feet high, and five hundred feet in length. *Torreones* (round fortifications) guarded two diagonal corners. The entire structure was as economical as it was simple and flexible.

Less than fifty men usually staffed these presidios, and they included four officers, a chaplain, and Indian scouts. Enlisted men served ten years. Recruits generally came from prison, their release being a useful military recruiting tool. They were uneducated, accustomed to poverty and were issued leather jackets and shields and wooden lances. Abused by officers, mistreated by their country, usually paid in goods rather than cash, constantly in debt, and buried wherever they happened to fall, the presidio soldier nonetheless set an example of bravery and endurance.

The tough, wiry, often unruly soldier did not fail the forts; the forts failed him. As a throwback to European warfare, the presidio flourished on the supposition that a fortification had to be assaulted and captured before an invading army could advance into enemy territory. A military post undestroyed theoretically could harass lines of communication, supplies and retreat. However, the Apaches never played this game. They rarely made frontal assaults, choosing instead to bypass the forts. So until after the turn of the century a stalemate existed. The Indians could not be defeated; the Spanish could not be expelled.

The Warrior Americans

BY THE EARLY 1800s, northern Mexico started retaining scalp hunters against the Indians. One was James Kirker, an Irish adventurer. Kirker could match the Apaches and Comanches terror for terror, treachery for treachery, and brutality for brutality. His bounty hunters, a vicious collection of Americans, Mexicans and Indians, noticeably thinned the Apaches. However, some states were often slow with scalp payments, Chihuahua Governor Angel Trías in particular having his moments of forgetfulness. There were also suspicions, not altogether unfounded, that the raiders sometimes substituted Mexican hair for Indian hair. Nobody could tell the difference, since one scalp looked about like any other when hanging from a grisly trophy pole.

Meanwhile, other events dramatically affected the Rio Grande country. Not only were Americans

Alexander Doniphan

moving in as traders and scalp hunters, the United States government assumed more interest in northern Mexican affairs. General James Wilkinson, who would become involved in Aaron Burr's alleged conspiracy to wrest the Southwest from Mexico, dispatched Lieutenant Zebulon Montgomery Pike to seek the source of the Red River. However, Pike strayed (intentionally, perhaps) from his assigned territory. When the Spanish arrested him as a spy, he was surveying near the Rio Grande. Soldiers brought him downstream in 1807, Pike therefore becoming the first known American military man to visit the Pass.

Twenty years afterward, Ponce de León, a wealthy Paso del Norte merchant, petitioned for land in what is now downtown El Paso. He built a modest home for his *mestizos*, and by the 1840s had added a few outbuildings. Folks called his place Ponce's Rancho.

During the 1840s, several Americans arrived at the Pass. T. Frank White operated a trading post at Frontera, a river crossing in El Paso's upper valley. Simeon Hart of New York built a grist mill squarely in the throat of the Pass where the Hacienda Cafe is today. James Wiley Magoffin of Kentucky lived in Mexico for years before becoming a trader hauling freight along the Chihuahua Trail, the upper Camino Real between Chihuahua City and Santa Fe.

He constructed a rambling hacienda called Magoffinsville near the present-day intersection of Magoffin and Willow streets about two miles west of Hugh Stephenson's ranch. Stephenson was a Kentuckian too, and he operated a trading post near what is now Concordia Cemetery.

El Paso was then in New Mexico, and Texas was six hundred miles to the east. As Spain and Mexico originally envisioned it, Texas had the Nueces River as its southern boundary. West Texas ended at about San Antonio. A few remote trails tied San Antonio in with Chihuahua.

After Texas won its independence in 1836, Mexican General (and President) Santa Anna signed the Treaty of Velasco, giving Texas something it had never had: the Rio Grande as a southern and western boundary. When safely back in his own country, Santa Anna repudiated the treaty and declared a state of war still existing. So Texas possessed on paper an extravagant boundary which in all instances it could not patrol, and in some instances could not even find.

The treaty relocated Ponce's Rancho (as well as Magoffinsville and Stephensonville) in Texas. Santa Fe was a Texas community, too.

Since Mexico did not recognize any of these paper acquisitions, Texas decided to at least bestow the blessings of economic, if not military, liberty on Santa Fe. In 1841, Texas launched its Santa Fe Expedition. Reputedly its members were traders, but there is ample suspicion that it was a military force as well. Within weeks the campaigners, lost and starving, surrendered to the Mexicans near present-day Tucumcari, New Mexico. The prisoners were walked through Paso del Norte on their way to Mexico City.

One hundred and eighty captives reached the Pass, the others having been shot or allowed to die of wounds, sickness or exposure. Captain Dámaso Salazar cut the ears off bodies and strung them on a strip of leather as proof that no one had escaped.

These Texans were the last foreign soldiers, if indeed they were that, to be seen in Paso del Norte until 1846. With the advent of the Mexican War, Colonel Stephen Watts Kearny left Missouri and easily took Santa Fe.

As Kearny moved west to capture California, Colonel Alexander Doniphan, a Kentucky lawyer, led the 1st Regiment of Mounted Missouri Volunteers south along the Chihuahua Trail. In one of history's most dramatic campaigns, these eight or nine hundred soldiers, undisciplined, out of uniform, hard-drinking, strung out for miles alongside the Rio Grande, reached Vado (then called Brazito) between what is now Las Cruces, New Mexico and El Paso, Texas. Here they encountered an armed force of approximately a thousand men, mounted and ready to contest the entrance to Paso del Norte.

As the Mexican army approached, a rider broke ranks and cantered toward the Americans. From a long, thin lance fluttered the black flag of No Quarter.

After brief negotiations during which neither side offered to surrender, the Mexicans charged. It was a short and decisive battle. The Mexicans were brave but poorly armed and led. They rode straight toward the crouched Americans and were blown away by intense rifle fire. The Missourians sustained only a few minor wounds. Mexican dead littered the battlefield. Having punched through the last resistance, Doniphan's dusty and victorious army marched unimpeded through the Pass and, two days after Christ-

After Texas won its independence in 1836, it possessed on paper an extravagant boundary it could scarcely patrol and in some instances could not even find. (Placido Cano)

mas 1846, peacefully occupied Paso del Norte. The north bank of the Rio Grande now slipped forever from the feeble grasp of Mexico.

When the Treaty of Guadalupe Hidalgo in 1848 terminated the Mexican War, the United States assumed awesome responsibilities toward its former enemy. The government agreed to help survey and mark the international boundary. It agreed to honor all Mexican land grants. It agreed to stifle all Indian raids into Mexico from north of the border. Furthermore, Washington accepted a responsibility to Americans. It would guard the boundary, defend the villages and towns, protect the immigrants, and safeguard the roads and trails.

By now Texas and the United States recognized the necessity for a wagon road connecting East Texas with El Paso. During the winter of 1848, Texas Ranger John S. Ford and Major Robert S. Neighbors, United States Indian Agent in Texas, opened a direct route from Austin to El Paso. At the same time, Lieutenant William H. C. Whiting of the Engineering Corps and Lieutenant William F. Smith of the Topographical Engineers surveyed a military road from San Antonio to El Paso. This route was called the lower road, whereas the Austin route became the upper road. Both had been blazed by midsummer, 1849.

Across these rutted, occasionally vanishing trails streamed thousands of covered wagons carrying forty-niners to the gold fields of California. With the traffic flowing almost exclusively east and west, El Paso recognized its economic opportunities, and gave up its New Mexico heritage by joining Texas. In 1850 El Paso County was formed. San Elizario became the first county seat.

Meanwhile, during the previous five years, Indian attacks had been increasing in New Mexico due to the reduction in armed forces after the Mexican War. Randolph Marcy, Secretary of State, believed better protection along the border could be achieved with a string of three or four forts along the Rio Grande between Santa Fe and Paso del Norte. On November 7, 1848, the War Department issued General Order No. 58, instructing the 3rd Infantry Regiment to take up station in Department No. 9, New Mexico. This would be the first American military post at the Pass.

The battle-hardened 3rd had just returned from Old Mexico. Washington sent a few companies to New Orleans Barracks, and then on to Santa Fe. The remainder went to Camp Salado, near San Antonio, Texas.

The latter consisted of the Regimental Staff and Companies A, B, C, E, I and K, plus a howitzer battery. Major Jefferson Van Horne, a slender, austere soldier who graduated number thirty in his West Point class of thirty-eight, assumed command. He was a forty-seven-year-old warrior, a veteran of the Indian campaigns in Florida, as well as the Mexican War battles of Contreras, Churubusco, Chapultepec and Garita de Belén.

Van Horne left Camp Salado on June 1, 1849 for El Paso. With him marched 257 soldiers, and a train of 275 wagons and 2,500 head of livestock. A horde of emigrants tagged along, forcing the caravan to move in small units to conserve water. Nevertheless, the travelers reached the Pass a hundred days later, pausing near present Tigua, five miles southeast of El Paso, on September 8, 1849.

On September 14, the Staff and Companies A, B, C and E (plus the band) moved into what was then Coons' Ranch, but is now the center of El Paso. On

Mexican lancers, patriotic and brave, faced Doniphan's rugged riflemen at the Battle of Brazito in 1846. (Antonio Castro)

the following day (September 15), Companies I and K and the Howitzer Battery left Tigua for San Elizario, twenty miles southeast of El Paso.

Benjamin Franklin Coons, merchant, developer and confidence man, learned of the government's plans for a post in the vicinity and purchased the Ponce de León land grant property for $18,000 shortly before Van Horne arrived. Van Horne's units needed quarters so Coons leased the main buildings and a six-acre tract to the Army for $4,200 a year. The tract comprised what is now the west portion of downtown El Paso, a region including the Plaza Theater, the Greyhound Bus Station, the Chamber of Commerce, and the Civic Center.

The site was simply a ranch comprising one large building and a few small adobe structures, an area so unimpressive that Van Horne did not consider it worthy of a description. He named his location "The Post Opposite El Paso," the "El Paso" referring to El Paso del Norte (now Ciudad Juárez), Mexico, the only large village nearby. He also referred to his post as being in New Mexico, because what is now El Paso County was then in New Mexico territory. During the latter 1840s, the area comprising Texas west of the Pecos was in dispute between Texas and New Mexico. The U. S. government considered it a part of New Mexico, and the post was placed in the New Mexico Department. It was not until 1850 that the 32nd parallel of latitude became the boundary line between Texas and New Mexico.

At the time of its establishment, the Post Opposite El Paso was the strongest military encampment in the Territory of New Mexico.

The Post
Opposite
El Paso

3

T HE ARMY at the Post Opposite El Paso was not
the stuff of popular legend. Infantry occupied this
site, an infantry based on the European concept of
warfare, an army carrying 1842 smoothbore percus-
sion muskets, the bright barrel finish adding emphasis to the eighteen-inch socket bayonet.

Nor were these soldiers typical American farm
boys. Over half were Irish and German emigrants,
men barely off the boat before being met by recruiting officers. These foreigners were generally
uneducated. They spoke broken English and more
than a few were hiding from wives and law officers.
They were the survivors of debtors prison, famine
conditions, and an oppressive foreign military draft.

At the Post Opposite El Paso, the recruits drilled

Some Fort Bliss soldiers, like these mounted riflemen, rode to battle but dismounted to fight. (Antonio Castro)

and planted gardens, drilled and gathered vegetables, drilled and constructed buildings, drilled and performed detail work, drilled and occasionally marched in futile pursuit of marauding Apaches.

While Van Horne had nominal command also of the Post at San Elizario, that garrison had an independent status. In spite of partial ruins, the rectangular presidio had suitable officers quarters as well as storage space. Except for Fort Marcy at Santa Fe, the Post at San Elizario was the only government-owned military facility in the Department of New Mexico.

The two posts had five missions: to entrench American authority firmly along the Mexican border, establish law and order where none existed, guard the Texas-New Mexico roads, provide escort service when needed for forty-niners and other travelers, and to intercept Indians intent upon raiding in the Texas-New Mexico Southwest or crossing the international line into Mexico.

As a practical matter, government employees tended to need the most help because there were so many of them. United States-Mexico Boundary Commissioner John R. Bartlett, 165 miles east of El Paso and thinking about eating his mules, wrote Major Van Horne on November 7, 1850, that his party was suffering greatly due to a severe snowstorm. He desperately needed additional mules, bread, pork, sugar, coffee and water, supplies sufficient to last five days until he could reach El Paso.

A bone-weary Bartlett then pushed on, only to encounter sixty government wagons and a herd of cattle stranded at the salt flats near the Guadalupe Mountains, a hundred miles east of El Paso. The train had left San Antonio nearly six months earlier in June, and had been stalled at the salt lakes for fifty-six days. Now, completely out of water except for the bitter-tasting stuff nearby, the train was unable to move forward or backward. Major Van Horne had been advised that oxen could not travel more than fifteen miles a day. As it would take six days to reach El Paso, barrels of water placed by the Army at strategic points along the road would enable the animals and travelers to survive. Van Horne responded with aid to both the boundary commissioners and the wagon train.

Van Horne also helped in more dramatic respects. Bartlett finally in El Paso, had no sooner welcomed his own wagon train than he dismissed teamsters with "bad habits and vicious dispositions." Most of them congregated at Socorro, fifteen miles southeast of El Paso, where they committed several murders and terrorized the town. By early January, 1851, the citizens and those boundary commissioners stationed there due to a housing shortage in El Paso, could stand no more. They captured three of the most dangerous, hauled them before a justice of the peace, and with a jury of six Mexican and six boundary employees, began a trial. In a sensational courtroom drama, with the jury, the judge and the spectators armed to the teeth, and with a snarling mob outside, a more likely atmosphere for additional bloodshed could not be imagined. At a crucial time, however, ten soldiers sent by Van Horne to keep the peace arrived, and with the military on guard, the trial came to a swift conclusion. The three were found guilty and hanged from trees in the Socorro Mission plaza. Another desperado was captured two weeks later, and hanged too. As might be expected, Socorro reverted to its peaceful ways.

Thus the returns (records) of both posts were filled with accounts of activity, if very little fighting. Units

Area map of the El Paso region. These are present day boundaries, and several towns and forts did not yet exist. Arizona was part of New Mexico. The Mexican border started west at Mesilla, so everything west of the Rio Grande, and between Mesilla and the present Mexican border, would be a part of the Gadsden Purchase. (Placido Cano)

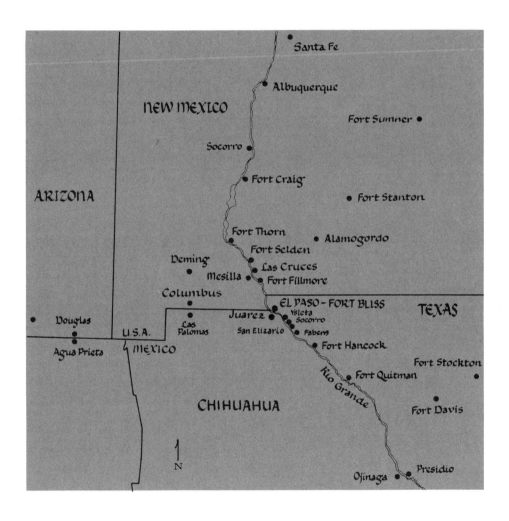

constantly marched from one post to another, producing dust and fatigue, but encountering few Indians. The treaty obligations with Mexico were particularly frustrating. The Americans had promised to deny entry into Mexico of hostile Indians or marauding outlaws. Yet, when these fugitives did slip across the Mexican border from the United States, Van Horne could not cross the line in pursuit.

Some tasks were once-in-a-lifetime endeavors, as when Company A spent two years escorting the boundary commission between El Paso and the Pacific coast. The gentle Lieut. Colonel Louis Craig was a constant companion to Commissioner John R. Bartlett until Craig's death while returning from California to El Paso. Craig tried persuading two Fort Yuma deserters into giving up, acknowledging their brutal treatment at the fort and promising to get them transferred to his command, if possible. Instead they murdered him. Fort Craig, New Mexico, was named in his honor.

By late 1850, eleven posts, like beads on a string, reached up and down the Rio Grande from San Elizario to Santa Fe. None of these seriously deterred the Indian, but all presented enormous supply problems for the soldiers.

In 1850 the country underwent an economy binge. Washington demanded more effectiveness with fewer men at less cost. To bring this about, Lieut. Colonel William Wallace Smith Bliss, Chief of Staff for General Taylor during the Mexican War and present Adjutant General of the United States Western Department, appointed Colonel George Archibald McCall as Inspector General.

McCall evaluated each post of the Department of New Mexico. He found few soldiers actually on duty.

Horses abandoned or lost by the Spaniards formed the nucleus of wild mustang herds. Comanches and Apaches swiftly became superior horsemen and for decades raided Rio Grande settlements. (Jose Cisneros)

"The Post Opposite El Paso" occupied the Coons' Ranch site – often erroneously referred to as Smith's Ranch. The post (shown in light gray) comprised what is now the northwest portion of downtown El Paso, a region including the Plaza Theater, the Chamber of Commerce and portions of the Civic Center. The asterisk identifies the Ponce de Leon hacienda location. (Placido Cano)

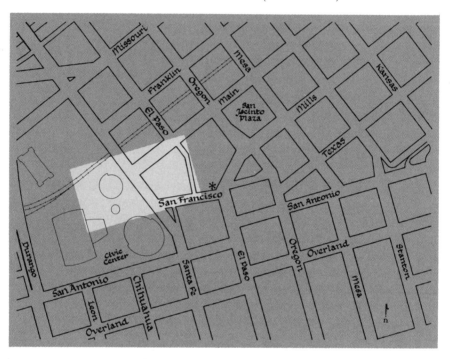

Only two posts out of eleven had over a hundred men present. The Post Opposite El Paso had eighty-one; San Elizario had forty-four.

His inspection report went for implementation to Lieut. Colonel Edwin Vose Sumner, commander of the United States Dragoons. Sumner vowed to revise the New Mexico defense system, to abolish garrisons near settlements, and to reduce the high operational expenses.

In September, 1851 the Post Opposite El Paso and the Post at San Elizario both closed. The soldiers were transferred to Fort Fillmore, near Mesilla, New Mexico, forty miles north of El Paso. This gave more protection to the Mesilla Strip, a thirty-five mile wide piece of land extending from the Rio Grande west to the headwaters of the Gila River. John R. Bartlett had given it to Mexico during boundary negotiations in the early 1850s, thereby forcing the United States to repudiate Bartlett's actions because the Americans needed the territory for a southern railroad.

In 1853, Secretary of War Jefferson Davis named Colonel Joseph K. F. Mansfield as the new inspector-general, and asked for a reevaluation of the western forts. Mansfield, whose report has become a frontier military classic, argued the need for more defense. In particular, he believed that a post near El Paso was indispensable. He suggested additional posts throughout West Texas to guard the trails from Austin and San Antonio. These proposals led to the creation of forts Lancaster, Davis and Quitman.

4 Fort Bliss

ON DECEMBER 1, 1853, Jefferson Davis, eventually to become President of the Confederacy, ordered a new military post at El Paso. By Christmas, Companies B, E, I and K of the 8th Infantry arrived from Fort Chadbourne, Texas. They were commanded by Lieut. Colonel Edmund B. Alexander, and he made the "Post of El Paso" official on January 11, 1854.

The post took up rented quarters at Magoffinsville, three miles east of Franklin (El Paso). Alexander chose this location no doubt because of better housing, and because he could more easily defend outlying ranches from a central position.

The Post of El Paso was where Magoffin and Willow streets intersect today. During those years, the Rio Grande formed several large curves in the vicinity, one of them establishing a partial perimeter

The 1st Dragoons and a regiment of Mounted Rifles made brief appearances at Fort Bliss during the mid-1850s. (Antonio Castro)

of the post. The buildings were of adobe, the walls forming practically a solid line near the sally port. The American flag waved from the central square. Army wife Lydia Spencer Lane, in her autobiography, *I Married A Soldier*, described the fort as "the most delightful station we ever had." She wrote of three adobe rooms and their dirt floors. "With canvas nailed down first, and a carpet over that, we were well fixed."

Two months later on March 8, 1854, the Post of El Paso officially became Fort Bliss in memory of Lieut. Colonel William Wallace Smith Bliss who died unexpectedly in 1853. While alive he never visited El Paso. Today the colonel's body rests on the military reservation which bears his name.

The 1st Dragoons and a regiment of mounted rifles made brief appearances at Fort Bliss during the middle 1850s. When campaigning, these units would ride to battle on horseback and then dismount to fight. The dragoons carried musketoons (sawed-off muskets), a nearly worthless weapon with a tendency for the ball to dribble out when the barrel pointed downward. By the late 1850s, the 1st Dragoons had been fitted with the new Sharps rifled carbine and a single-shot, muzzle-loading horse pistol.

But infantry still dominated military thinking, and during late April, 1857, soldiers from Fort Bliss assisted in the Gila River campaign in New Mexico. Although not an operation of inspiring strategy, twenty-four Indians were killed and twenty-six captured.

To the north of Fort Bliss, a twisting, boulder-strewn passageway known as Dog Canyon was developing its terrible reputation. It gashed the western slopes of the forested Sacramento Moun-

Fort Bliss at Magoffinsville in 1857. The flag is oversized, and the Franklin Mountains have had some liberties taken with their location. The nearby Rio Grande is not shown. The site today is at the intersection of Magoffin and Willow streets. (Aultman Collection, El Paso Public Library)

tains near what is now Alamogordo, New Mexico. In July, 1858, Lieutenant William K. Jackson and Company D from Fort Bliss pursued Mescalero Apaches into Dog Canyon and recovered several horses and mules. They took one prisoner. Good fortune did not smile another time as Lieutenant Henry M. Lazelle led thirty men of Company D into the canyon and a disastrous fight on February 8, 1859.

Meanwhile, El Paso had a population estimated at three hundred. The Plaza (as it was known then), or Pioneer Plaza (as it is known now) was in front of where the Plaza Theater is today. An irrigation

Lieutenant Colonel William Wallace Smith Bliss. Although a brilliant officer, and son-in-law of President Taylor, he never visited El Paso, or the post which bears his name. (Millard McKinney Collection)

ditch paralleled San Francisco Street and watered the cottonwood and ash trees. Beneath their shade old folks relaxed, young lovers promenaded, and vendors peddled tortillas and tamales.

On Sundays everyone usually gathered in the plaza and listened to the Fort Bliss regimental band play melodies by Stephen Foster. Forty-niners awaiting an opportune time to move out would shout for "Westward Ho." Somebody always wanted to hear "Ben Bolt" too, and the audience loved rous-

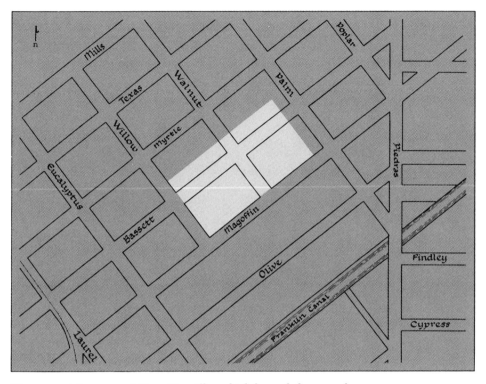

The present day area of Magoffinsville, which housed the second military post in El Paso (1853-1868). This is the first location identified as Fort Bliss. (Placido Cano)

ing tunes such as "Blue Tail Fly," "Turkey in the Straw," and "Buffalo Gal." Concerts usually ended with "My Old Kentucky Home," guaranteed not to leave an Anglo dry-eyed in the crowd.

Nevertheless, the specter of whether a country could remain half slave and half free was already haunting the nation. Its pall lay everywhere, being present during plaza activities, for all men sensed that dark and controversial times would engulf even El Paso.

The Fight
at Dog Canyon

UPON LEARNING that Apaches had stolen several head of cattle and three mules at San Elizario, Lieutenant Henry M. Lazelle and thirty men of Company D, Mounted Rifles, left Fort Bliss on January 31, 1859, and rode twenty miles to San Elizario. They were joined by several citizens of that town, a guide and an interpreter.

The Indians had a three-day start and were headed easterly along the "Old Salt Trail" through rocky terrain near present-day Tornillo, Texas. Southeast of there, they turned north and skirted the east side of the Hueco Mountains.

After riding 165 miles in seven days, a weary Company D, nearly out of water as the Indians had stripped it from the water holes, reached the entrance of Dog Canyon. It was twelve miles south of present-day Alamogordo, New Mexico, a deep slash in the western slopes of the Sacramento Mountains. For two-and-a-half miles the Company followed the winding, rock-strewn trail, the path at times so narrow that men and horses squeezed by in single file. The soldiers finally emerged onto a broad plain surrounded by high mountains where they encountered thirty armed Apaches raising a white flag and asking to talk.

The discussion was fruitless, and that night Lazelle led twenty-two men to where he could overlook the Indian campsite. However, when dawn came, the Indians were three-fourths of a mile further up the canyon.

Indians ordinarily did not stand and fight, but these had been reinforced and now outnumbered the troopers three to one. They also controlled the high ground.

Skirmishes started. Lazelle forced the Indians from several positions until, being outflanked and down to twelve rounds per man, he ordered a withdrawal. Four men carried out Private Newman whose hip was fractured. Private Ogden was killed as he helped bear Newman. Then Private Stamper was hit, and Newman was shot in the head. The retreat continued, easing somewhat when the troopers reached the narrow ledges where the Indians would not attack from the flanks. (According to Lazelle's report, the Indians did not roll rocks down upon the soldiers as has so often been stated.) When Company D reached the desert floor, the Apaches broke off.

A mounted trooper rode ahead to Fort Fillmore, near Mesilla, New Mexico. On the evening of the next day, a bedraggled Company D was met at San Agustín Springs by Major William Gorden and the 3rd Infantry.

Three troopers had died in the dramatic skirmish. Five were severely wounded, including Lieutenant Lazelle. The Apaches lost nine men. And so ended the largest pitched battle ever engaged in solely by Fort Bliss troopers during the Indian wars.

5 The Rifles of War

THE ISSUE OF SLAVERY never really surfaced at the Pass. Not more than a half-dozen slaves (including those belonging to army officers) ever walked the dusty streets at any one time. Usually a black man was a "servant." El Paso contained few slaves since there existed no need for plantation labor. Also, with the town's proximity to the river, slaves could merely cross the Rio Grande to freedom.

In El Paso the issue was States' rights, and Southerners (who made up the bulk of the Anglo residents), were adamant about it. Each afternoon they met in Ben Dowell's Saloon, where the Paso del Norte Hotel is now, and loudly denounced the government. In terms of a debate, the disputes had a certain repetition since nearly everybody shared the same point of view. However, the discussion always heated during the presence of the Mills brothers, Anson and William Wallace. Each man had strongly influenced the town's growth, but each was as arrogant as he was articulate. Now they supported the Union, and being unloved anyway, they had enemies everywhere.

Anson and W. W. were at a disadvantage since Fort Bliss on December 8, 1860, had been shifted out of the Department of New Mexico (a strong Union territory) and assigned to the Department of Texas. Departmental commander General David Emanuel Twiggs was one of the Army's three full brigadiers, a vindictive, white-bearded tyrant who sympathized with the South. Being unable to get any clear directives from Washington, he surrendered all U.S. military installations in Texas to state authorities before the Civil War even started. On February 18, 1861, Fort Bliss property was turned over to James Magoffin, who owned the land and buildings anyhow. The public funds went to Simeon Hart. Altogether Fort Bliss lost a twelve-months' supply of subsistence and ammunition for approximately two companies.

Only the Fort Bliss commander, Colonel Isaac V. D. Reeve, and Lieutenant Lazelle remained loyal among the officers at Fort Bliss. The Mills brothers repeatedly urged Reeve to ignore Twiggs, to march his troops to Fort Fillmore, near Mesilla, and remain there in Union Territory until receiving definite orders. But Reeve suffered a shortage of backbone and a lack of ability to make decisions. Anson Mills, a former student at the U.S. Military Academy, then fled to Washington and accepted a commission in the Army. W. W. Mills slipped into Paso del Norte exile and became a Union spy. However, Simeon Hart had him kidnapped off the Mexican streets and imprisoned at Fort Bliss. Mills remained there until escaping and joining the Union in northern New Mexico.

These were times of transition. Enlisted men did not have the privilege of resignation. If a soldier left before his five-year enlistment expired, he was a deserter. However, officers could resign their commissions, and one of many who did so was James Longstreet who had served brief terms as Fort Bliss commander, and who would build a towering military reputation during the Civil War. He brought his family to El Paso from New Mexico, leaving them in town to await a wagon train while he went on ahead to join the South.

On March 31, 1861, Reeve ordered the Stars and Stripes lowered over Fort Bliss. He and the 3rd Infantry Regiment, consisting of 134 men, marched out of Magoffinsville and started down the rutted road heading east. Along the way, the garrisons at forts Quitman and Davis joined them. Together these soldiers were supposed to walk to the Gulf coast and take ship to the national capital. However, they were arrested near San Antonio, and spent the Civil War in Texas confinement.

The 2nd Regiment of Texas Mounted Rifles (volunteers) under the command of Confederate Colonel John R. Baylor reoccupied Fort Bliss on July 1, 1861. The balding, argumentative, forty-year-old Baylor was an Indian fighter who kept his three hundred frontiersmen in line and who limited military plundering to what he considered reasonable limits.

Baylor's only Union opposition awaited at Fort Fillmore, forty miles north along the Rio Grande. There Major Isaac Lynde and his 7th Infantry Regiment of six hundred men debated their options. They were in Union country, surrounded by hostile pro-Southern civilians openly urging the Army to desert. So greatly did this undermine Lynde's confidence, that when Baylor moved his smaller force within striking distance on July 25, Lynde abandoned the post and fled across the San Andres Mountains. He surrendered that same afternoon at San Agustín Springs, presently within two miles of command headquarters at White Sands Missile Range.

A week later on August 1, Baylor declared himself governor of the Territory of Arizona. In those days New Mexico included what is now Arizona, but due to the large distances involved in traveling to Santa Fe on territorial business, a serious proposal called for cutting the giant area roughly in half along the lines of latitude 34° North. Mesilla would be the capital. Although the idea never caught hold, when Baylor captured Mesilla, on his own volition he recognized the Territory of Arizona. It thus became the only Confederate Territory of the war.

Meanwhile, Confederate President Jefferson Davis dispatched Brigadier General Henry Hopkins Sibley, an ailing visionary who spent too much time with the liquor bottle, to Fort Bliss. Sibley had hopes of utilizing El Paso as a base for conquering New Mexico and California, and perhaps even annexing portions of northern Mexico. All he need do was destroy the Yankees in New Mexico, and a portion of his dream would be within reach. But to do that, he would have to defeat Colonel Edward Richard Sprigg Canby, commander of the Department of New Mexico, a determined fighter.

Sibley reached Fort Bliss on December 14, 1861, and invaded New Mexico in early February 1862. Two months later the Confederate campaign crested at Glorieta Pass near Santa Fe. Sibley was defeated and chased toward El Paso. By early July, the final Confederate units had forsaken Fort Bliss for East Texas after attempting to burn the post. They left a makeshift military hospital intact with twenty-five of their wounded and sick inside.

In Sibley's wake the post fell to the cold-eyed Colonel James H. Carleton and his California Column, a Union fighting force of 2,350 men that had skirmished its way eastward across New Mexico until reaching the Rio Grande. By early August 1862, Company C of the 1st California Volunteer Cavalry was camped at Hart's Mill. On the 16th, Carleton arrived with Companies B of the 1st and 2nd California Volunteers. The colonel paroled the sick Confederates at Fort Bliss and sent them to San Antonio.

Carleton also took command of the Department of New Mexico, which included Fort Bliss, transferring his headquarters to Santa Fe where he replaced Canby who was being called to Washington. Carleton left a young and dapper Major William McMullen in charge of Fort Bliss which was now a shambles. As James Magoffin and most Southern sympathizers had fled to East Texas, even Magoffinsville had fallen into decay. Consequently, McMullen spent most of his time at the former post of San Elizario guarding the nearby river crossing. McMullen suspected the Texans of plotting another invasion, approaching El Paso from the Mexican side of the Rio Grande.

With the United States preoccupied by Civil War, France invaded Mexico. Maximilian, the Archduke of Austria, became emperor, forcing President Benito Juárez north to Paso del Norte. French legions followed him to Chihuahua City where they stacked their rifles, hesitating to risk provoking a strong and hostile American presence in and around Fort Bliss.

At the beginning of the Civil War, the Stars and Stripes were lowered over Fort Bliss. The blue-clad 3rd Infantry Regiment marched out of the Magoffinsville post, and the post was occupied three months later by Texas troops. (Antonio Castro)

Thus a weak Mexican federation continued to survive. From his Santa Fe headquarters, General Carleton "condemned" quantities of small arms and ammunition, leaving them in designated locations along the international line where Mexican forces could find them. Carleton also offered asylum at Fort Bliss for Juárez and his officers, saying, "You must believe that in your reverses you have our deepest sympathy."

The Mexican president refused to leave his country, and within a short time had defeated the French and regained his office. And so it happened that years later in September, 1888, Paso del Norte, once the president's temporary home in exile, was renamed Ciudad Juárez, the City of Juarez.

With the Civil War over, a military government nominally headquartered at Fort Bliss exerted its power over El Paso. Nobody traveled without a military passport. Weapons were severely restricted, registered with the Army. An evening curfew existed. Military tribunals supplanted county and district courts. Confederates such as Magoffin, Hart and Ben Dowell were charged with treason, their property auctioned from the Plaza.

Yet, the Army had little heart for civilian chores, and by 1865 the Southwest started returning to normal just as if the Civil War had been but an interlude. By October the California Column began mustering out. On the 15th, the 5th Infantry Regiment of Army regulars marched into Fort Bliss, officially replaced the volunteers, and formally raised the U.S. flag. The post, which had reverted to the Department of New Mexico, now came under the Department of Missouri.

Camp Concordia

UNITED STATES MARSHAL Albert H. French, acting as a private citizen, purchased Magoffinsville for $4,000 in December, 1865. (The courts would later return the hacienda to its rightful owner, James Magoffin.) French then rented out portions of Magoffinsville to the army for use as Fort Bliss. The post thus remained where it had been since 1854.

Following the Civil War, four black regiments were formed, the 124th and 125th Infantry and the 109th and 110th Cavalry. These units were originally designated United States Colored Troops (USCT) and all of the enlisted men were black and the officers were white. In July 1866, the War Department established the regiments in the Regular Army as the 24th and 25th Infantry, and the 9th and 10th Cavalry.

On August 12, 1866, elements of the 25th Infantry

relieved the 5th Infantry at Fort Bliss. Companies G and H of the 25th served during a period of relative Indian peace, their greatest excitement coming in May 1867, when the flooding Rio Grande washed away storerooms and portions of the officers quarters. Most of the garrison entered tents and the Army considered moving the post to higher ground.

The 25th Infantry transferred to Santa Fe two months later, being replaced by Companies A and K of the 35th Infantry, a white regiment. On November 21, the 35th received orders to move onto a hundred acres of Concordia Rancho, property leased from the old Hugh Stephenson estate. Even so, Fort Bliss at Magoffinsville was not abandoned until March 1868 when Camp Concordia was completed.

Camp Concordia had three large adobe buildings that straddled three major roads, two leading to San Antonio (one through Hueco Tanks, the other through Fort Quitman), the other pointing north toward Tularosa, New Mexico, pioneering what is now Dyer Street (U.S. Highway 54). The location of old Camp Concordia is immediately south of Interstate 10, across from Concordia Cemetery.

The Rio Grande was less than a mile south of Camp Concordia, the drinking, washing and cooking water being brought daily to the post in a water wagon. Three men and eight mules handled the chore. Military reports claim that once the water had been filtered and settled, it became comparatively pure and usable.

Of the three buildings, one contained eighteen rooms, the others twelve and eleven. Ceilings averaged fourteen to sixteen feet high. There were six adobe officers quarters, plus a tree-lined parade ground. Though the soldiers planted a garden, grew fruit trees and even had a vineyard, all watered by a

U. S. Cavalryman at Fort Bliss during the 1870s. (Antonio Castro)

nearby *acequia* (irrigation ditch), Camp Concordia was a terrible place to live. The post lay in a bed of sand and gravel. Rains created a quagmire; droughts formed huge cracks in the hard earth.

Black infantrymen usually garrisoned the camp during those years, years spent hunting the Apache chief, Victorio, who roamed the Southwest and Mexico. (Victorio would finally be slain by Mexican soldiers at Tres Castillos, Chihuahua, roughly 150 miles due south of El Paso.) American troops marched for weeks at a time, crossing hundreds of dusty, thirsty miles, enduring hardships beyond belief, and rarely sighting an Indian. Only mounted soldiers had a chance of catching the Apaches, and even these were rarely that successful. Companies of the black 9th and 10th Cavalry frequently stopped at Camp Concordia either to take up station for a short time or to pick up supplies.

At isolated Camp Concordia, the old days were gone, the days of social gatherings, parties and band concerts in the Plaza. Those would not have been available to black troops anyhow, but even the white officers now had few places to socialize as most civilians concentrated on rebuilding instead of attending fandangos. Companionship for soldiers meant a dance hall called "The Bucket of Blood" half-way between Magoffinsville and Camp Concordia, about where Piedras and Alameda streets join today. There a soldier could find easy love or a murderous fight. Between the venereal diseases and deadly brawling, plus the increasing incidents of malaria and pneumonia at Camp Concordia, this post was not the happiest of frontier locations.

On March 11, 1869, Camp Concordia was re-designated Fort Bliss. Within the decade, however, tough economic times plagued the nation, and the

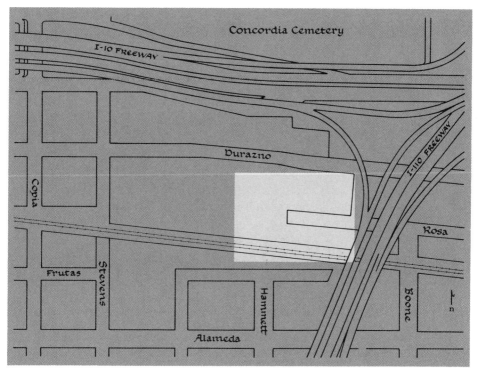

The third Army post in El Paso was Camp Concordia (1869-1876), a temporary name for Fort Bliss. It was immediately south of today's I-10, and across from the present Concordia Cemetery. (Placido Cano)

government sought ways to reduce military expenses. It solved part of its financial problems by again abolishing Fort Bliss in January, 1877.

Had the government not been so anxious to reduce expenses, it might have avoided the tragedy known as the El Paso Salt War. The struggle had been brewing for years as El Paso politicians sought to collect fees for salt taken by Mexicans from beds lying beneath the shadow of Guadalupe Peak, a

57

hundred miles east of El Paso. Initially the violence had limited itself to political killings, the murders becoming more serious when attorney Charles Howard shotgunned his partner, Judge Luis Cardis. Cardis had supported the Mexican cause, and his death aroused the Mexican people in San Elizario. They threatened to take salt with or without Howard's permission. The resultant insurrection was not easily contained. Even a company of Texas Rangers surrendered to a San Elizario mob, the only such capitulation in history. Colonel Edward Hatch, commanding the District of New Mexico, rushed to El Paso from Fort Bayard and assumed command of Troop L of the 9th Cavalry and Companies A, G and I of the 15th Infantry, all being from Bayard and Fort Davis, Texas. The cavalry troops were black and known by the Indians as "buffalo soldiers." When several columns of these grizzled warriors, dressed in full battle gear, went trotting into San Elizario, the Salt War ended immediately without further bloodshed.

Colonel Hatch remained in El Paso long enough to investigate and write a report about the Salt War. In a letter dated January 11, 1878, he made the following recommendation: "The remedy for the disturbance in this region is the establishment of a military post. Had there been a garrison of even a hundred men at Fort Bliss, it is not likely the present trouble would ever have occurred. As long as the frontier remains as it now is, and there is little probability of its changing, troubles of a like nature, or even more serious, are likely to occur..."

Congress had already authorized the reestablishment of a military post at the Pass. Fort Bliss would rise again like a phoenix, this time on New Year's Day, 1878.

Fort Bliss
at Hart's Mill

7

COMPANY L of the 9th Cavalry and Company C of the 15th Infantry reoccupied old Camp Concordia, then in ruins. After futile attempts to repair it, the troops rented quarters in downtown El Paso, drilling in the Public Square, now San Jacinto Plaza. This was the Post's fourth location, and troops remained in "Garrison Town" for two years. Oddly, Company L remained a cavalry outfit without horses until August 30, 1878 when forty-five animals finally arrived.

Yet it was monotony that got to the men. John F. Finerty, correspondent for the *Chicago Times*, came out of Mexico into El Paso during April, 1879, and he described Fort Bliss officers as looking "worn and melancholy." The soldiers "yawned and complained of the station, damned the eternal heat and flies, cursed the bad water and inveighed against the sandstorms." They longed for action, he said, and

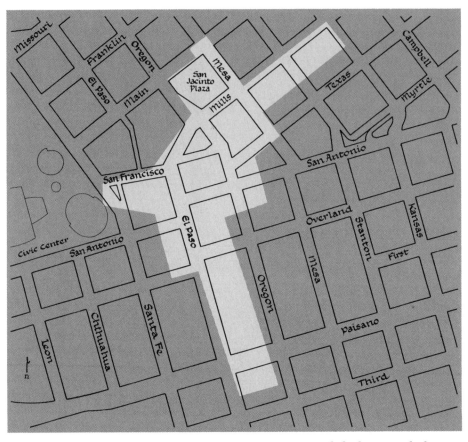

The post's fourth location (1878-1880) provided El Paso with the nickname "Garrison Town." The Army rented abandoned downtown buildings, and the troops drilled on El Paso Street, as well as in the Public Square (San Jacinto Plaza). (Placido Cano)

would welcome the roughest kind of frontier service to "the torrid tranquillity of Ft. Bliss."

As the post needed better accommodations than those found in empty downtown warehouses, a board of officers examined several potential sites. It settled on 135 acres alongside Hart's Mill.

To hold down construction expenses, the Army

60

El Paso Street when Fort Bliss troops drilled on it. Thank goodness none of the soldiers were barefoot. (Dom Bernardi, MBank)

used military labor. In December 1880, all was ready. Most of the buildings were of masonry, adobe and wood. The roofs were shingled. Officers quarters and enlisted mens barracks all had porches, and for the first time the post had a separate hospital building.

General of the Army William Tecumseh Sherman

Black cavalrymen were called "Buffalo Soldiers" by the Indians, a phrase of respect given by one warrior to another. Troopers from the black 9th and 10th Cavalry frequently made Fort Bliss home during the Indian Wars. (Jose Cisneros)

suggested that the name Fort Bliss be retained. Secretary of War Alexander Ramsey made it official on July 18, 1879.

As a frontier post, Fort Bliss caused little excitement. On occasions it seemed deserted, as in May, 1888 when only seventeen soldiers were on active duty. The post was a way station for soldiers shuttling back and forth to the Arizona Indian wars, for Geronimo was loose and running along the international border. In September, 1885, Lieutenant Britton Davis of the 3rd Cavalry, and his chief of scouts, Al Sieber, brought sixteen Apache scouts along when they visited Fort Bliss.

Sometimes there would be a few hours of excitement and even tragedy. In May 1887, fire destroyed portions of the post. Twenty-eight horses died in the inferno.

The Hart's Mill site did have its drawbacks. The Rio Grande formed the western boundary of the post. During cloudbursts the water would foam and roar as it rushed through the Pass on its way to the curves just a mile or so away. With moisture so close, the eddies collected the usual mosquitoes. Drinking, cooking and bathing water came from the murky river. Silt refused to completely settle out, and the soldiers suffered from dysentery. The post surgeon repeatedly complained about unhealthy conditions.

The railroads arrived in 1881, bringing headaches for Fort Bliss when the Santa Fe laid track across the center of the parade ground. The Southern Pacific passed on the east perimeter of the post.

The trains compensated for disturbing the military routine by loading and unloading passengers and supplies within the fort itself. So while tracks

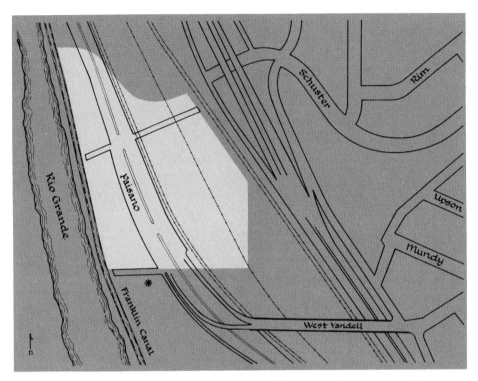

The post's fifth location (1880-1894) was on the property of Simeon Hart. The Rio Grande flowed alongside. Asterisk designates Hart's Mill. Only one corral was outside the light gray area. (Placido Cano)

across the parade ground were a nuisance, the inconvenience alone did not necessitate abandoning the post. Obviously the site was too small for growth, and any fort that could not grow would eventually be phased out. Largely through W. T. Lanham, El Paso's representative in Congress, the city began pressing the War Department for a much larger military post.

The Post
on the Mesa

AS THE INDIAN WARS faded, the need for small, scattered frontier outposts vanished. The Army had become so successful that it had no one else to fight. It seemed on the verge of putting itself out of business.

The 1880s called for different priorities. Expensive and isolated posts would have to be reevaluated. Mobility no longer depended solely upon the horse. Iron rails could transport soldiers to distant trouble spots. In return, the Army would protect the railroads.

Modern plans called for the consolidation of obscure military posts into large, regional forts accessible to railroads. In this respect, El Paso's geographic position gave it an advantage over better known Arizona, New Mexico and Texas forts that had practically become household words during the Indian wars — Fort Defiance, Fort Union, Fort Huachuca, Fort Apache, Fort Davis. El Paso dominated the strategic gateway into and out of Mexico. The town showed possibilities of becoming a regional population center, and most importantly, from the military's point of view, it was at the confluence of five different railroads promising the rapid transportation of soldiers around the Southwest.

General William T. Sherman, Chief of Staff of the Army, assigned General Phil Sheridan, commander of the Military District of Missouri, to evaluate the West Texas-New Mexico region for a main fort. As nobody in Washington thought in terms of building a new post, but only of expanding or updating an older one, Sheridan recommended Fort Selden (established in 1865), fifteen miles north of Las Cruces and alongside the Rio Grande. While Sheridan believed El Paso to be the most logical site, he argued that Fort Bliss could not be expanded due to the Rio Grande and Mexico on the west, and a string of low lying hills to the east. The Army could never quarter large numbers of troops at Fort Bliss.

Sherman endorsed Sheridan's judgment, but in 1882 made a military tour himself during which he stopped in El Paso in late March. There he became convinced that while Fort Bliss might be tiny, it was too strategic to be replaced by Fort Selden. Sherman believed that with careful planning, Bliss could be expanded into a regimental infantry post. Cavalry units could be stationed at Fort Cummings, New Mexico, between Deming and Hatch.

With conflicting opinions about which fort to rebuild, Congress appropriated a small amount of money each for Fort Bliss and Fort Selden. Then the matter rested for the next few years as the Geronimo campaign flared again in Arizona.

By 1887, Fort Bliss had entered the Department of Arizona, then shifted into the Department of Texas where departmental commander Brigadier General David S. Stanley tried to get Fort Bliss expanded or relocated. He argued that Fort Bliss could be too easily intimidated by hostile forces occupying a range of hills directly across the Rio Grande in Mexico. He also called attention to the cramped space for the construction of new buildings and the bisection of the parade ground by the Santa Fe Railroad. Stanley referred to fumes emitting from a nearby smelter, and claimed they were hazardous.

The military's renewed interest in Fort Bliss stimulated a corresponding excitement by local citizens. The El Paso Development Board (Chamber of Commerce) took up the cause with a thirteen-page pamphlet entitled "El Paso as a Military Post." It gave emphasis to the drive and on March 1, 1890, Fort Selden lost the battle when President Benjamin Harrison signed a $150,000 authorization for a new Fort Bliss within ten miles of El Paso. It would house a twelve-company garrison on 300 to 600 acres.

However, the bill underwent revision. A second reading showed the money could be spent only for construction. The land would have to be donated.

El Paso geared up for the purchasing and contribution of some six hundred acres of land out on the mesa, at a site called "Lanoria," from the Spanish *la noria*—"the well." Nor were El Pasoans too upset when the Army upped its request to a thousand acres. That was still within reach. Anson Mills, in town arousing interest in his international dam at the throat of the Pass (which later went to Elephant Butte), stoutly supported the idea of a new and larger military fort. Partly at his suggestion, the

El Paso Progressive Association was organized. It would carry the financial burden of raising money for the land purchase on Lanoria Mesa.

The location cost El Paso citizens $8,700 for the thousand acres. That wasn't enough. The Army wanted positive assurance of available water. El Pasoans drilled a well and struck crystal clear water.

El Paso had shown good faith. It had done more than its share. It had kept the commitment. But there was more to come.

Captain George Ruhlen of the Quartermaster Corps, left Washington, D.C. and arrived in El Paso to inspect the new military site. After a brief examination, he shocked the town. The purchased land did not include the mesa's southwest edge, the region now extending from Pershing Gate to Howze Gate. If Fort Bliss did not have possession, undesirable elements would establish businesses there beyond military control.

El Paso's land acquisition committee believed it had already gone beyond any reasonable demands, but as the additional amount was only fifty acres, once again the public rose to the challenge. The land would be used for a string of officers quarters (now Officers Row), and would furnish a suitable location for a road entering the reservation. The El Paso committee obtained the necessary land, and again settled back to await the construction of a huge military post.

But the Army was still not satisfied. It insisted that El Paso acquire two hundred acres more, a demand nearly sending citizens into cardiac arrest. After an exchange of several harshly worded letters with the Army, the town raised the money, although not as easily this time. The Army now had

Troops such as this cavalry sergeant were constantly transferring into and out of Fort Bliss in 1899. (Antonio Castro)

1,266 acres for a new Fort Bliss, and for the time being seemed content.

Contracts for construction went out in June, 1892, for this would not be a post built with troop labor. Yellow brick and limestone were the most common building materials. While much of the unskilled labor came from El Paso, the contractors imported men and materials. Laborers earned $1 a day, carpenters $3, bricklayers $6. A surveyor was paid $160 monthly. Brick cost $8 a ton.

Work began in September. Soon the mesa resembled a small city as contractors temporarily furnished living quarters for workers. By February, 1893, the initial construction was complete.

The 18th Infantry from Fort Clark, Texas, became the first occupants. Regimental Headquarters, the band and Companies A, C, D and H comprised a garrison of 225 officers and men who arrived on October 27, 1893. The figure, large by Fort Bliss standards, still fell short of the twelve to sixteen companies anticipated during the fund raising campaign. Colonel Henry Lazelle, commanding officer of the 18th Infantry and previously stationed in El Paso, was scheduled to take charge, but the colonel was on sick leave in Minnesota. The honor of first commander fell to senior officer Captain William H. McLaughlin, a fifty-year-old career man with twenty-six years in grade.

Old Fort Bliss at Hart's Mill then went to the auction block, and by 1895 it had been practically sold. The Army also owned a former post cemetery located in what is today the Public Library block and Cleveland Square. That area was donated to the city.

In some respects the old tune "Happy Days Are Here Again" might have applied to Fort Bliss-El

Paso relations although such good rapport primarily existed between the officers and the upper-class civilians. Ordinary soldiers and ordinary civilians tended to remain at arms length. The first known social event took place during the Christmas season, 1892. Major James Henton, commanding officer of Fort Bliss at Hart's Mill, invited a hundred distinguished civilian guests to the new post for a picnic in honor of a Miss Bates and a Miss Mc-Donald, guests of Miss Josephine R. Magoffin. The visitors moved back and forth to Bliss and town through the courtesy of the White Oaks Railroad. The tracks passed a few hundred yards east of the present intersection of Dyer and Tompkins streets. Everybody took buggies for the quarter-mile to the post.

And although the fort was a long five miles from town, "officer meets girl" often continued to apply. In late 1896, Lieutenant William Jefferson Glasgow, aide-de-camp to the Department of Texas Commander, married Josephine Richardson Magoffin, daughter of Joseph Magoffin, judge and five-term mayor of El Paso. The Immaculate Conception Church on Myrtle Avenue at Campbell Street overflowed with family, friends and well-wishers.

The 18th Infantry Band averaged four evening concerts a week, some on post and the remainder in El Paso. Colonel Daingerfield Parker, who assumed command of Fort Bliss during 1895, demanded the best band in the Army. He got it by arranging the transfer of especially competent musicians to his post. In June he arranged a musical performance in the Myar Opera House to raise funds. The event received intense advance publicity, but when the day came, not a single El Pasoan purchased the twenty-five and fifty-cent tickets. Reasons might have been the depressed economic conditions or that residents were conditioned to hearing the regimental band free of charge. Whatever, an infuriated Parker built a $560 bandstand at Fort Bliss and vowed that the military band would never again play in town. It didn't either, not until Colonel D. D. Van Valzah replaced Parker in early 1896.

In April, 1895, Fort Bliss lost Companies A and C, transferred to Fort Sam Houston following enormous wind damage to Bliss. In their place, Fort Bliss received Troop A of the 5th Cavalry. This mounted unit would be permanent, so the War Department authorized the construction of additional stables.

At this point, the military at Fort Bliss stabilized until April, 1898, when during the Spanish American War the 5th Cavalry departed for the fighting zone. The 18th Infantry regiment left for New Orleans soon afterwards. El Pasoans gave them a thunderous, cannon-booming, flag-waving sendoff, emotional because El Pasoans were dearly proud of their country's actions in Cuba. However, that left Fort Bliss temporarily with one officer and four enlisted men manning the entire post. Even the canine mascot "Dewey" was transferred.

Troop F of the 1st Texas Volunteer Cavalry reoccupied Fort Bliss on July 29, but due to several rowdy elements, a relationship never warmed with the townspeople. After several fights between soldiers and civilians, and more than a few jailings, El Pasoans did not mourn the cavalry's departure for San Antonio in late September. Company C of the 3rd Texas Volunteers replaced them, and did not fare any better. It left the post in early 1899.

What happened next sorely tested those El Pasoans with high hopes for an enlarged Fort Bliss. With the war over, Company A of the 25th Infantry Regiment marched into Bliss, a unit with blue uniforms, polished boots and black faces. Since Civil War days the 25th had garrisoned far-flung Texas posts, had laid telegraph wire, built roads, and fought Indians. It boasted of a commendable record in Cuba.

El Paso enthusiastically welcomed the troops. Fort Bliss had accommodated black soldiers before. The town also had a black civilian contingent of roughly two percent of the total population. Many were professional and business people, and their community standing was excellent.

Yet, racial antagonisms between civilians and black soldiers soon engulfed the town. Policemen arrested "Black Fannie" and Corporal Samuel F. Dyson for drunkenness. Early the next morning on February 17, 1900, a half-dozen soldiers stormed the jail and killed officer Newton Stewart, an ex-Rough Rider. Jailer Dick Blacker, asleep when the shooting started, grabbed a revolver and drove the attackers off, killing Corporal James H. Hull. Fort Bliss soon produced three men for civilian trial, all from the 25th Infantry. Of these, Sergeant John Kipper, twenty-five years old, was accused of being the leader. His trial commenced on May 1. A week later the jury sentenced him to life imprisonment. Not long afterwards, a higher court reversed the conviction and sent Kipper back to court. Again a jury gave him life. He served ten years before Texas Governor O. B. Colquitt pardoned him.

With civilian-military relations strained, El Paso gave no wild sendoff to the 25th Infantry Regiment when it transferred to the Philippines in mid-May, 1901. It was replaced by sixty-nine members of the 12th Cavalry, all white.

The 25th returned in late 1905, and in a relatively minor incident which demonstrated the strained emotions, Mayor Charles Davis caned a Fort Bliss sergeant in February, 1907 for interfering when Davis summoned a policeman to arrest an intoxicated private. These were unfortunate times made worse by racial tensions engulfing Texas and the Southwest. Whites had been deeply affected by the Brownsville, Texas riots where black soldiers had mutinied. Because of the incident, feelings ran so high in the South that the War Department transferred many Negro troops to the Philippines. The 25th left El Paso in early March, 1907.

Fort Bliss languished for the next few years as a prevalent rumor had it being abandoned and the soldiers transferred to Fort Sam Houston in San Antonio. While this never happened, the War Department hesitated to enlarge Fort Bliss, giving an excuse that a huge post, while serving no useful purpose to the Army, might alarm a friendly Mexico. As a mollifier, the Administration assigned the 19th Infantry, an all white regiment to Fort Bliss.

Since its inception, the new Fort Bliss had been remote from town, the five miles of rutted road discouraging all but the most determined. The first known thoroughfare followed what is now Pershing Drive out to Dyer Street, then north to Tompkins. At that point it crossed the White Oaks Railroad tracks, later the EPSW (El Paso and Southwestern Railway, now the Southern Pacific) and entered the post at North Gate, now Forrest Road. By 1900, however, a wagon road came out that same Pershing Drive until it struck a steep incline. Buggy riders then got out and pushed until entering South Gate, now Pershing Gate.

After the turn of the century, more effort went into establishing better local contact with Fort Bliss. The roads were graded. In 1906 an electric streetcar

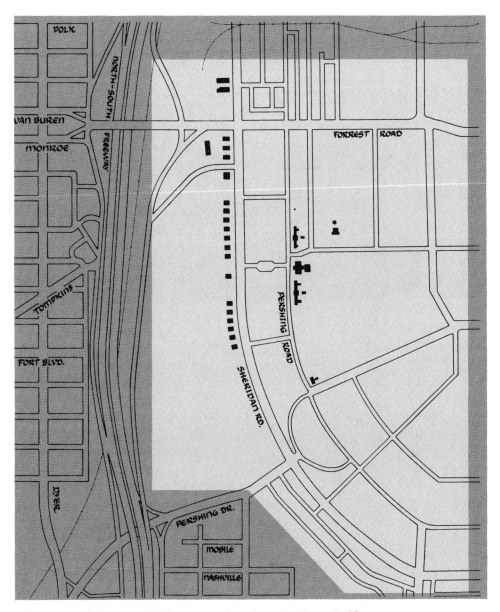

The post's sixth location (1893 to present) on Lanoria Mesa. Buildings and quarters as originally constructed (1893) are shown. (Placido Cano)

began operating between town and Fort Bliss. Business increased so briskly that within two years, the streetcars were averaging five trips daily. They even grabbed the mail contract, replacing the military wagons.

All the while, the only large military commitment at the Pass came in late 1909. Thousands of soldiers, mostly from forts Sam Houston and Clark, and housed in boxcars, demonstrated a formidable display of power for presidents William Howard Taft of the United States and Porfirio Díaz of Mexico. Four regimental bands added color to the various parades. Out at Fort Bliss, the military entertained Secretary of War Jacob M. Dickinson, the commanding officer of the Department of Texas Brigadier General Albert L. Meyer, American Ambassador to Mexico David E. Thompson, Governor Thomas M. Campbell of Texas, and Mayor Joseph Sweeney of El Paso.

But military units come and military units go, and the 19th Infantry departed for the Philippines in early 1910. Fort Bliss drifted toward caretaker status. Though the army showed no inclination for closing the post, it gave no hope of enlargement.

Meanwhile, across the border, revolutionaries with fiery rhetoric and a multiplicity of firearms were threatening to sweep away the government of Mexico. The forthcoming violent Mexican upheaval would involve the United States in its fury. In the American response, Fort Bliss would begin its long, slow climb from an isolated post into one of the nation's foremost military installations.

Mexican Border Troubles

E<small>L PASO IN</small> 1910 had the largest Mexican community in the United States, fully 10,000 of the nearly 40,000 population being of south-of-the-border descent or parentage. Of these, many were Mexican political exiles, revolutionaries, men and women with fierce and burning eyes who considered neither the cost of their forthcoming insurrection, the practicalities of their struggle, or even their ultimate goals. They united only in their hatred of President Porfirio Díaz, expressing their murky ideals through dozens of Spanish-language newspapers and broadsides, most of which never became financially strong enough to last beyond two or three issues.

El Paso itself had modernized. A few streets were already paved, citizens no longer drank water from the Rio Grande, electric lights and gas and telephones were becoming common fixtures. There were schools, a library, a few theaters. Gunfighters such as Dallas Stoudenmire, John Selman and John Wesley Hardin were but a short time dead, as the city tried to rise above its violent past. Officers became policemen instead of marshals. Mining, smelting, railroading and agriculture were the dominant industries. In 1907 the city had adopted a charter, and switched from the ward system to councilmen elected at large. Fort Bliss was still important to the city's economic stability, although as yet too small and too far removed from town to be a decisive economic influence in local growth.

As political and military events in Mexico continued to deteriorate, revolutionaries began gathering northwest of Ciudad Juárez across the Rio Grande from ASARCO Smelter. The tough, American-appearing Brigadier General Pascual Orozco brought fifteen hundred guerrillas out of the remote Chihuahua mountains and camped them alongside the river in April, 1911. With Orozco's immediate aim the capture of Juárez, his chances improved considerably with the arrival of forces led by a little-known bandit chieftain, Pancho Villa. These combined insurgents would be commanded by the wispy scion of wealthy Mexican parents, Francisco I. Madero. As a liberal and intellectual, he understood his people; as a politician he dominated the Mexican scene; but as a military leader, he had scarcely a trace of ability.

In early 1911 Washington quietly reinforced Fort Bliss with infantry units from Fort Douglas, Fort Huachuca, and Whipple Barracks, all in Arizona. By February, with insurgents across the river, Fort Bliss commander, Colonel A. C. Sharpe of the 23rd Infantry, ordered continuous twenty-four hour, four-man patrols alongside the Rio Grande near the smelter, Hart's Mill, Washington Park, and the four international bridges. *The El Paso Times* assured El Pasoans on February 3, that Fort Bliss soldiers formed an unbroken line from the smelter downstream fifty miles to Fort Hancock. These soldiers were present to keep spectators away from the international boundary when the assault on Juárez commenced. As it was, during the battle for Juárez from May 8-11, 1911, stray bullets caused seventeen American civilian casualties. Juárez fell to the insurgents.

With the capture of Juárez, the subsequent sailing into exile of President Porfirio Díaz, and the election to the presidency of Francisco Madero, El Paso and Juárez reverted to tranquil cities. The 23rd Infantry Band played weekly concerts in Cleveland Square and other parks.

As a larger military payroll began making its presence felt, the Chamber of Commerce renewed efforts to enlarge Fort Bliss. It reminded Washington of promises made almost twenty years previously. The city wanted a regimental post. Now was the opportune time for Washington to redeem its commitment.

For a few weeks the possibilities looked promising. Secretary of War Henry L. Stimson and Army Chief of Staff General Leonard Wood visited El Paso and Fort Bliss. Neither seemed openly optimistic about El Paso's chances for an enlarged post, but they thought it a goal worth pursuing. That was sufficient encouragement, and the city council passed a resolution allowing the United States government to install and maintain a ten-inch sewer pipe from Bliss to the municipal lines.

A month later, in November 1911, Fort Bliss officially became a cavalry post. The army began construction of four more stables and started wiring a Fort Bliss electric lighting system, completing it in January, 1912.

Meanwhile, Colonel Edgar Zell Steever, Jr., of the 4th Cavalry feared for the uneasy peace between the two countries. American citizens had been threatened in Mexico, and the El Paso city council called for an invasion of its neighbor to the south. However, even the council seemed to realize the foolishness of its motion, recognizing that any invasion might lead to a possible massacre of Americans stranded inside the Mexican interior.

As it was, the 23rd Infantry was transferred to Indiana in early January, 1912. That left only the 4th Cavalry to patrol the border and guard the international bridges.

During early February, the Mexican political and military situation worsened as Madero insulted Pascual Orozco by denying a high political office to the courageous but administratively incompetent guerrilla leader. Orozco fumed and then rebelled, joining nearly two thousand insurgents gathered near Juárez who opposed the Madero presidency. As Steever ordered the 4th Cavalry into positions along the Rio Grande, Juárez quietly surrendered to the rebels. A disappointed El Paso press dubbed it "a battle that wasn't."

To retake Juárez, Madero dispatched his most able general, Victoriano Huerta. He recaptured the city with as much ease as it had been lost.

Even with the situation calm, the War Department still took no chances. Three batteries of the 3rd Field Artillery and the entire 22nd Infantry arrived at Fort Bliss. These units would guard the international bridges, and patrol the border from the smelter to Washington Park. During 1912, the garrison at

Revolutionaries sharing a tender moment between battles. Soldiers for both sides usually brought wives and children. (Leon Metz Collection)

Fort Bliss increased to three thousand men, up a thousand from a year earlier. An average of $100,000 a month entered the El Paso economy on paydays. Hundreds of soldiers browsed about El Paso streets during off-duty hours.

Tensions took a frightening twist in Mexico as General Huerta seized the presidency himself and arranged Madero's murder. This brought Pancho Villa out openly against Huerta, although it took him a while to escape from a Mexican jail where Huerta had him imprisoned. Villa entered temporary exile in El Paso where he brooded, bought a motorcycle, ate ice cream, and slowly gathered an army. In early January, 1914, he reentered Mexico and captured Ojinaga across the Rio Grande from Presidio, Texas.

Villa's assault changed the nature of the Mexican Revolution's effect on El Paso. Mexican refugees had previously been absorbed by El Paso relatives, or they had rented El Paso hotel rooms. While these refugees gave the city a large floating Mexican population, it was a population mostly housed. When Villa took Ojinaga, however, thousands of panicked refugees and Federal soldiers crossed the river to Presidio and surrendered to the U.S. officer in charge, Major M. M. McNamee. McNamee promptly exhausted his supply of blankets and tents, so he marched his Mexican charges to the rail station at Marathon, Texas and shipped them to El Paso. General Hugh L. Scott, commander of the Southern Military District, assured the city that the prisoners would be incarcerated on Fort Bliss. They would not be released to wander about town.

For four months the Army imprisoned between 4,000 and 5,000 refugees, a figure rising and falling as relatives and camp followers came and went.

Armed guards patrolled the grounds. The compound was encircled by three fences of barbed wire. However, as many people escaped "into" the compound as escaped out. Those inside at least had food and shelter.

For all of its efforts, the Army could not completely reassure El Pasoans that hordes of poverty-stricken refugees would not soon be released to descend upon them. In May, 1914, Scott relocated the majority of the prisoners to Fort Wingate, New Mexico.

Back in Mexico, Huerta's opposition called themselves Constitutionalists. As Huerta had taken over the country by illegal means, the new faction demanded a return to constitutional government. The most powerful names included Venustiano Carranza of Coahuila, Alvaro Obregón from Sonora, Emiliano Zapata from Morelos, and Abram González and Francisco Villa from Chihuahua.

The Constitutionalists laid siege to Chihuahua City. They also attacked Zaragoza, Mexico, ten miles downstream from Juárez.

As a precaution against an overflow of fighting into the United States, the American army shuttled Troop M of the 13th Cavalry from Columbus, New Mexico, to Fort Bliss. A tightening of guards and patrols took place at the international bridges. To discourage Americans from entering the war zone, the government required passports before returning to the United States. The order slowed traffic and hindered legitimate business activities.

During 1913, in one of the boldest and most brilliant military actions of the revolution, Pancho Villa captured a southbound train near Chihuahua City, boarded it with an army of two thousand men plus horses, and forced the engineer to steam back to Juárez. There in the pre-dawn hours of November

Pancho Villa, on horse, gives encouragement and battle instructions to rebel soldiers. (El Paso Public Library)

15, the train rolled quietly into the city. When citizens awoke that morning, they no longer belonged to the Federal government. Old scores were settled as groups of Federal sympathizers were rounded up, marched to the cemetery and executed.

Juárez had now changed hands for the fourth time since 1911, and though this capture was quiet by revolutionary standards, occasional bullets did cross the river and strike El Paso stores, saloons, hotels and homes. One person was wounded.

Out at Fort Bliss, General Hugh Scott established his headquarters. He would command the El Paso

Military District until early 1914. In particular he attempted to militarily seal the border. At Ysleta, ten miles southeast of El Paso, soldiers discovered over four hundred head of horses and large quantities of riding equipment, material being stockpiled for a Federal assault on Juárez. A week later, unidentified persons poisoned water holes near Ysleta, killing numerous American cavalry horses. Someone killed an American private with a blow on the head and threw his body under a U.S. railroad bridge. Grim-faced El Pasoans watched the flag-draped coffin carried through city streets to Union Station.

In April, 1914, General John J. Pershing assumed command of Fort Bliss when he arrived from San Francisco with the 8th Infantry Brigade, which included the 6th and 16th Infantry Regiments. Although the two regiments comprised nearly five thousand troops, and they took up quarters at Camp Cotton, an area bound by Cotton Avenue on the west, present Paisano Drive on the north, Cordova Island on the east, and the Rio Grande on the south.

Pershing bedazzled the people of El Paso with a gigantic parade to demonstrate how well the Pass was protected. As the city fathers declared "Army Day," he smartly marched nine troops of the 13th Cavalry, seven troops of the 15th Cavalry, four troops of the 12th Cavalry, and the entire 6th, 16th and 20th Infantry Regiments, Battery B of the 3rd Field Artillery, Batteries A, B and C of the 6th Field Artillery, and seven military bands. El Paso had once wanted a regimental post. Now it had something akin to a divisional post.

Among other things, this armed force would become an agent for social change. Infantrymen

patrolling the river near *Chihuahuita* (Little Chihuahua, being named for the poor Mexican emigrants who had come out of Chihuahua to live
there), complained about unsanitary conditions in
the area. Calling the situation a menace to the
health of his soldiers, Pershing prevailed upon the
city council to order nearly 150 adobe shacks
demolished.

Conditions in *Chihuahuita* still deteriorated so
Pershing placed his entire medical corps at the
disposal of Mayor Tom Lea. During the next few
months the Army in cooperation with the city Board
of Health, periodically swept through the narrow
streets, hosing out the filth, gathering up the dead
animals, burning the refuse, and even tearing down
a few structures. In those days such high-handed actions were not considered social sins.

South of the border, Pancho Villa had come upon
difficult times. He and the constitutionalists had
rolled south into Mexico City, sent Huerta into exile
and at their moment of triumph began to fall out
among themselves. The power struggle ended with
Carranza and Obregón jointly pushing Villa back to
Chihuahua where they could contain him though
they could not defeat him.

Over in the United States, Victoriano Huerta
dreamed of a reentry into Mexico. He chose El Paso
as the site. However, U.S. marshals learned of his
coming and arrested him and Pascual Orozco on a
train at Newman, Texas, roughly twenty-miles
north of El Paso and alongside the New Mexico state
line. Both men were charged with violations of the
neutrality laws. After making bond, Orozco fled
into the Big Bend country of Texas where a posse
killed him a short time later. Meanwhile, the
government was suspicious of Huerta's intentions,

and hesitated to bring him to trial for fear he would be released. Huerta was under house arrest in El Paso before being transferred to Fort Bliss. There he was placed under guard in a building formerly used as quarters for hospital stewards. He remained at Fort Bliss throughout the summer and fall while his family took up residence at 415 West Boulevard, now West Yandell. When the ruthless old warrior learned of Orozco's death, the will to live slipped from him. Never one with scruples about drinking, he consumed more and more liquor as his health steadily declined. On November 7, 1915, he was released to his home where, after two hospital operations for cirrhosis, he died on January 13, 1916. His body was placed in a holding vault at Concordia Cemetery for twenty years. Today his remains are buried in El Paso's Evergreen Cemetery.

Villa too had reached the pinnacle of his career. Of all revolutionary leaders, his name alone became a household word in Mexico and the United States. El Paso newspapers praised his abilities. General Pershing met him on the international bridge in August, 1914, and personally escorted the military chieftain for a review of Fort Bliss. It was followed by a reception at Quarters No. 1, today known as the Pershing House (228 Sheridan Road).

By autumn El Paso housed perhaps the largest body of troops in the nation. No "for rent" signs existed anywhere. However, heavy traffic had reduced the two roads from town to Fort Bliss into what the newspapers described as "miserable" thoroughfares. Secretary of War Lindley M. Garrison and Army Chief of Staff General Leonard Wood wondered aloud if El Paso, considering the condition of the roads, really wanted to retain Fort Bliss. In mid-December the county agreed to pave the highways. There was even talk of all-night streetcar service.

Ceremonial and sporting functions galore now started at Fort Bliss. The post celebrated Mother's Day with bands and a mixed chorus of servicemen, plus young ladies from the First Presbyterian Church and the YWCA. For Memorial Day the Army invited to the post members of the Grand Army of the Republic, Confederate Veterans, Daughters of the American Revolution, Daughters of the Confederacy, and the Spanish American War veterans. Fort Bliss formed an army league baseball team, and the 20th Infantry won the championship. The 4th Artillery football team defeated the State School of Mines (now the University of Texas at El Paso) by two touchdowns. The 16th Infantry soccer players thumped the United Empire Club of El Paso, while the 6th Infantry sergeants consistently outshot the El Paso Police Department.

For its part the city administration bowed to military pressure and closed the midtown red-light district, usually called the Tenderloin. Broadway, the predominate street, later was renamed South Mesa. Even so, the city was not prepared to go all the way in its cleanup. Mayor Tom Lea instructed the police to ignore working girls south of 8th Street.

The year 1915 ended tragically for General Pershing as his wife and three of his children died in a fire at the Presidio in San Francisco. And as El Paso entered 1916, the period became just as tragic for the United States and Mexico. On January 10, sixteen American engineers were removed from a train at Santa Ysabel, Chihuahua, and executed—allegedly by Villa partisans. When the bodies reached El Paso three days later, the town went berserk. Several hundred civilians, augmented by numerous

In May 1911, hundreds of El Pasoans thronged to the Rio Grande, across from the smelter, to watch gathering rebel forces prepare for the first assault on Juarez. (Leon Metz Collection)

soldiers, rumbled out of the saloons and beat Mexicans wherever they could be found. Local police could not control the mob, and four companies of Fort Bliss infantry finally dispersed the crowds. No one was killed, but numerous heads were bashed.

Villa denied responsibility for the Santa Ysabel massacre, but the murderers had been members of his forces, if not units directly under his command or responding to his orders. Guilty or not, Villa was indicted by the American press and American public opinion. President Woodrow Wilson, his Mexican foreign policy already in a shambles and not having hit bottom yet, made motions to recognize

Carranza as the legitimate president of Mexico. If that happened, Villa would be nothing but an outlaw.

In a desperate effort to avoid the inevitable, Villa rallied his rag-tag army for one more campaign. He would invade Sonora. By controlling that giant state, plus Chihuahua, he would dominate all of northwestern Mexico. Then the United States would have to regard him as more than a minor figure in Mexican affairs. However, the invasion floundered. Obregón's troops in Sonora defeated Villa at every clash. And while Villa was on the trail, Wilson recognized Carranza.

A bitter and frustrated Villa headed north, fleeing the Sonorans and hoping to get satisfaction against the Americans. Early in the morning of March 9, 1916, Villa's forces crossed the international line and stormed the sleeping village of Columbus, New Mexico, changing history forever.

Seventeen American soldiers and civilians died in that assault. By early morning, after Villa had retreated back across the border, the United States and Mexico looked across the abyss of war.

President Wilson's frustration stemmed from Mexico's inability to maintain the responsibilities of a stable nation. Due to this the United States government considered Mexico neither equal nor inviolable. Prior to 1916 Washington had behaved toward Mexico with remarkable restraint. Now it would treat its neighbor like an irresponsible child. For the first time in nearly three-quarters of a century, the Americans would invade, not to conquer a territory but to do for Mexico what it seemed unable to do for itself—establish stability in Chihuahua.

El Paso would have been the most logical invasion route for a punitive expedition. The El Paso-Juárez complex had railroads, highways and a back-up supply system. Yet, due to Mexican emotionalism, a crossing into Juárez might have drawn sharp fighting, as both Mexican civilians and the government agreed on opposition to the American entry. Pershing therefore moved south from the relatively isolated town of Columbus, New Mexico. On March 15, he led his forces on a remarkable odyssey into Chihuahua. Pancho Villa disappeared into the mountains.

Shortly after the punitive expedition entered Mexico, the Michigan and Georgia National Guard brigades arrived in El Paso and occupied Camp Cotton. These units would assume border patrol duties, and in particular walk guard duty at the international bridges as well as the railroad bridges at the smelter.

El Pasoans now expressed concern about their military protection being depleted even though General Frederick Funston, commander of the Southern Department, assured the city that adequate soldiers remained for defense. These assertions did not satisfy Mayor Tom Lea who saw Mexican revolutionists everywhere. He and *The El Paso Times* kept a running drumfire of criticism toward Wilson's Mexican policy.

On April 30, 1916, General Hugh Scott and Funston met General Alvaro Obregón in Juárez to discuss matters of mutual concern. As Carranza's representative, Obregón wanted the Americans out of Mexico. Later, Obregón and Scott met privately in El Paso at the Paso del Norte Hotel. Together they worked out a highly conditional plan for a Pershing gradual withdrawal, an arrangement that Wilson endorsed and Carranza tentatively approved. But nothing ever came of it.

During that same month, Mexican raiders crossed the Texas border and struck Glen Springs and Boquillas, both in the Big Bend country of Texas. Many El Pasoans continued to worry that the city might be attacked, so on May 10, in a show of force, two companies of infantry moved out of Fort Bliss and camped near the new courthouse being constructed downtown. To further soothe the population, and to send a message to Mexico, a massive parade took place on Flag Day, June 14. Twenty-five thousand soldiers and thousands of civilians marched through the streets. A sham battle took place in Washington Park. Civilian spectators packed it to capacity.

Nor was there any lessening of military troop movement to the Pass. Battery A of the New Mexico National Guard Artillery with one hundred men and four three-inch guns arrived in late June. Regiments from Georgia, South Carolina, New York, Michigan, Pennsylvania and Illinois followed. Massachusetts and New Jersey guardsmen reached El Paso in early July. Altogether El Paso had about forty thousand soldiers. These included regulars of the 8th Cavalry, 82nd Field Artillery, 20th Infantry, the 5th Field Artillery, and the 2nd Battalion of the 4th Field Artillery. News reports described El Paso as having the largest body of soldiers ever assembled at one place in the United States since the Civil War.

News reports also pointed out other things, such as an account of the Michigan band tramping through the Georgia tent area of Camp Cotton while playing "Marching Through Georgia." Outraged Southern boys came boiling out of their tents, and the greatest mass fist fight ever seen in El Paso roared out of control for several minutes. Bloody noses, bashed heads and broken knuckles kept the doctors busy for hours,

The first meeting of General Alvaro Obregon, left, Mexican Federal Army; General Francisco Villa, center, commanding the Northern Rebel Army; and General John J. Pershing, right, commanding Fort Bliss and El Paso Military District, at the Santa Fe Street Bridge in El Paso on August 16, 1914. Behind Pershing's left shoulder is his aide, Lieutenant James L. Collins, father of Astronaut Michael Collins. (Leon Metz Collection)

but nobody was killed in the free-for-all. Tension stayed tight for the next few weeks as officers kept the Northern and Southern boys separated. And the bands neither played "Dixie," "Marching Through Georgia," nor any other tunes calculated to offend the regional sensibilities of various military units.

Late in July twenty-six thousand regulars and guardsmen, with dozens of bands, assembled for a parade twenty-five miles long in El Paso. Mayor Lea declared a holiday.

Meanwhile, American soldiers with Pershing did

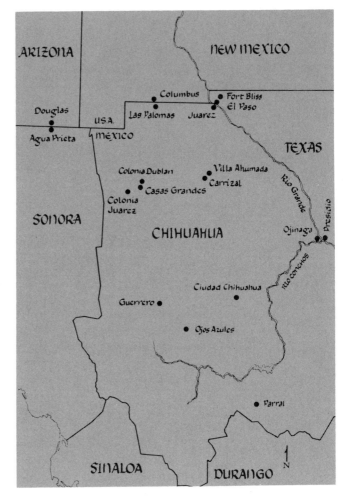

Pershing's expedition into Mexico. Map shows area covered by American troops in Chihuahua searching for Pancho Villa. (Placido Cano)

little except march back and forth across the desert while fighting brief skirmishes at Parral, Guerrero and Ojos Azules. On June 21, 1916, Troop C and Troop K of the all-black 10th Cavalry fought a major battle, the debacle at Carrizal, about a hundred miles due south of El Paso.

Although the battle inflamed public opinion in the United States, instead of expanding the Punitive Expedition, Wilson had already made up his mind to terminate it. Considering restrictions placed on Pershing (do not enter large towns, do not pursue farther south than Parral, avoid the trains, get clearance before making major decisions), the general had done all he could in Chihuahua from a military point of view. True, he had not captured Villa, which might have been fortunate. Had the wily guerrilla been taken prisoner, the Americans could neither have released him, shot him, turned him over to the Federal government, or removed him from the country for trial in U.S. courts. In short, Villa was an embarrassment while loose and running; he would have been a dilemma had he been caught. What actually took place, and not what latter-day historians believe should have happened, is the true reality of the Punitive Expedition.

At this point in history, Wilson perceived Germany as a greater threat to peace than Mexico. He ordered Pershing to begin withdrawing by January 31, 1917. By February 5, nearly all American soldiers had exited at Columbus. Left behind was a stronger and more popular Villa, a man able to humiliate the Federals until the central government, through bribes, finally retired him to a ranch near Parral where Villa became a gentleman farmer before being assassinated by Mexican enemies in 1923. Mexican factions continued to bicker, and occasionally shoot at each other for another two decades until a strong central government finally asserted itself.

José Gonzalo Escobar, an ambitious cavalry officer had commanded the Federal garrison at Juárez during 1919. He had risen through the ranks to brigadier general and had led a cavalry charge against Pancho Villa. In 1919, he lead the unrest against former president Plutarco Elias Calles, who politically and militarily dominated the country.

The Escobar revolt began on Sunday, March 3, 1929, as generals and colonels rebelled in ten Mexican states. However, insurgent control of Juárez had top priority. Not only could the rebels extract loans, tap banks and collect all the import and export duties, they could easily get supplies. Furthermore, they could simply cross the Rio Grande and place themselves under the protection of the American Army at Fort Bliss if the battle went against them.

Juárez had a small peacetime garrison commanded by General Manuel J. Limón, the only military leader in Chihuahua who refused to abandon his government. General Matías Ramos from Mexico City arrived to assist him. For the time being at least, as Escobar struggled to hold the revolution together in the south, the Chihuahua insurgent forces would be led by Governor Marcelo Caraveo, a unique Escobar supporter who remained loyal to the end.

Caraveo sent two thousand rebels and two generals, Miguel Valle and Agustín de la Vega, to capture the town. The army reached Samalayuca, thirty miles south of Juárez, by train, and then marched across the sand hills to the border city because Limón had destroyed the tracks.

Over at Fort Bliss, General George Van Horn

Moseley sent a warning to Caraveo through the United States consul in Chihuahua City. Moseley threatened "necessary action for protection" of American life and property in El Paso. Caraveo replied that he would regret any international incidents, but as Juárez Federal troops were not capable of defending the city, pretensions in that regard would "make them exclusively responsible for difficulties with the United States." He had a point.

On Friday morning, March 8, 1929, the battle commenced as thousands of El Pasoans clustered under a warm sun to view the struggle from roof tops and river levees. The *Literary Digest* called El Paso "the only section of the United States trained to appreciate warfare as a neighborhood spectacle." By 10:30 a.m. the rebels had pushed the Federals to the Rio Grande. By 12:30 p.m. General Moseley had become an intermediary. He arranged for Mexican Federal troops to take asylum at Fort Bliss. Thus generals Limón and Ramos, their staffs and troops, families, baggage, horses and some motorcars, crossed the Santa Fe Street Bridge, checked in with Immigration authorities, and were transported by truck to Fort Bliss. The Mexicans kept their own guns, but surrendered the ammunition. They also posted their own guards. After nearly a month at the post, the soldiers shipped out by Southern Pacific to Naco, Arizona, where they crossed the Mexican border and assisted the Federal government forces.

Total casualties had been light at Juárez. About three hundred government soldiers had surrendered or deserted to the rebels. Another three hundred turned themselves over to the Americans. Nine had died in the fighting, and seventeen were wounded. An American bartender at the Mint Cafe in Juárez was shot as he slept at the St. Louis Hotel. Over in

El Paso, a three-year-old girl was killed and a seven-year-old boy wounded, each by stray bullets. The First National Bank and its fifteen floors drew fire, forcing management to transfer employees downstairs.

Oddly, the successful attack on Juárez sounded the death knell of the Escobar revolt. The rebels had been beaten almost everywhere, and various subordinates grumbled that Escobar seemed capable only of retreating, destroying railroads, sacking banks and making newspaper statements. Desertions became epidemic, partly because of what the press called the "$50,000 cannonball," an agreement whereby the Federal government bought the command of a rebel general for a price which included amnesty for the rebel leader. Although Escobar arrived in Juárez within days following its capture by Caraveo, the Federals were so close behind that the general judged his military position as desperate. He retreated west to Sonora by train where he suffered additional defeats before crossing the border into the United States and going into Canadian exile. He did not return to Mexico until 1942.

Today there is hardly an official Mexican pronouncement which does not make reference to the Revolution. The Revolution seared the Mexican psyche as nothing has before or since. All in all, a painful era in North American relations, though swiftly forgotten by most of the United States, remained a bitter Mexican memory well into modern times. •

The Charge at Carrizal

DUE TO THE STUPIDITY and personal rivalry of commanding officers, the British in 1854 lost one-third of a unit during the foolish battle of Balaklava in the Crimea. Alfred Lord Tennyson immortalized that incident in his famous "Charge of the Light Brigade.

A reasonable parallel can be drawn at Carrizal, Chihuahua, about a hundred miles south of El Paso. In an unimportant, unnecessary engagement, American forces lost one-third of Troop C and K of the 10th Cavalry, all black soldiers except for officers.

On June 17, 1916, the brave but not particularly resourceful Captain Charles T. Boyd, of Troop C, led fifty-one men from Casas Grandes on a scouting expedition toward Villa Ahumada. Approximately one hundred miles separated the two, with Carrizal being in between and roughly fifteen miles south of Villa Ahumada.

Boyd interpreted his orders to march *through* Carrizal, rather than go around. Near this remote hamlet he was reinforced by thirty-six men of Troop K, led by Captain Lewis S. Morey.

On the morning of June 21, the combined cavalry units approached the adobe town with its twenty or thirty flat-roof buildings sitting atop an open plain. Ranking officer Boyd sent a message to the Federal commander, General Félix U. Gómez, noting that the American units were on a peaceful mission. He asked for permission to pass through Carrizal.

When Gómez denied the request, Boyd brought his cavalry to within a few hundred yards of the town and dismounted them. They began an advance which turned into a charge, and as the Americans reached the first mud walls, rifle and machine gun fire raked the troopers.

Boyd took a bullet in his hand, led a charge at the gun position, suffered still more wounds, and fell dead across the emplacement. Lieutenant Henry R. Adair assumed command and overran a defensive position. When he backed off to find ammunition, a bullet struck him in the heart.

An elderly lady living in Carrizal told this

writer that as a little girl she witnessed the Battle of Carrizal. She recalled seeing a wounded Mexican soldier run to her father's well. She thought it very funny at the time, for as the soldier drank water, it poured out through a hole in his throat.

Meanwhile, Morey's Troop K, covering the flank, became disorganized after Morey himself was wounded. The soldiers retreated in an "every man for himself" route. A few men were lost in the desert and were not found for days; a few others surrendered to Mexican troops and were promptly shot.

In this largest battle of the Punitive Expedition, the Americans suffered forty-four casualties. The Mexicans, out of an estimated force of three or four hundred, lost approximately fifty killed and fifty wounded. General Gómez lay among the pile of dead.

Captured Americans were removed to the Chihuahua City prison. Negotiations started immediately for their release, and within days they had been repatriated by train to Juárez where they walked across the Santa Fe Street Bridge into El Paso.

Today at Fort Bliss Charles T. Boyd and Henry R. Adair are commemorated by streets named in their memory. Back in tiny Carrizal, a one-room schoolhouse honors General Félix U. Gómez.

It is too bad that another Lord Tennyson has not arisen to give immortality to the brave Mexican and American soldiers who fell during the most senseless clash of the Punitive Expedition—Carrizal.

10 The Great War

EL PASO has always been a military town but seldom to the extent of 1916 and 1917 when fifty thousand soldiers flooded the Pass. More soldiers than civilians were seen on the streets, with the servicemen being quartered in Fort Bliss, Camp Baker, Camp Beirne, Camp Cotton, Camp Courchesne, Camp Fabens, Camp Pershing, Camp Stewart, and Camp Ysleta. Smaller outposts existed at Washington Park, Anapra, the cement plant, Globe Mills and the Santa Fe Street Bridge.

By early 1917 National Guard troops began returning home. The Pennsylvanians alone filled thirty cars of a troop train. Michigan soldiers occupied almost as many. When these soldiers went home, only about eleven thousand bored troops remained in the local area. Idle Americans had more time to think about themselves and their relationship to the community. Irritations previously ignored surfaced and festered. What happened was substantially documented in numerous letters to the *El Paso Herald*.

Soldiers accused merchants of price gouging. They claimed civilians treated them with contempt. And of course the civilians censured the soldiers for drunkenness, vile language, and being offensive to decent women. To make matters worse, the regulars and guardsmen feuded among themselves, each blaming the other for bad public relations.

Meanwhile, responsible soldiers and civilians interacted to reduce friction. The Army invited El Pasoans to the post for sporting events, parties and parades. The downtown people sponsored social clubs and organized dances. The city built Fort Bliss a swimming pool. When an army chaplain complained that a restaurant had refused service to three soldiers in uniform, the El Paso city council indignantly passed an ordinance forbidding such discrimination.

In 1916, streetcar motormen struck, and when replacement workers took over in June, riots began. Rampaging strikers, supported by scattered soldiers, overturned cars, smashed windows and beat recently hired motormen. Fort Bliss sent provost guards to clear soldiers from the area, and the mob became even more ugly. Mayor Tom Lea and former mayor Charles Kelly climbed aboard overturned cars and gradually calmed the crowd.

Most civilians believed soldiers spent too much time in saloons. Already the voice of reformers thundered throughout the land, and in El Paso nobody needed any more reforming than the military. Not only were the troops being led astray by liquor, but by brothels. The soldiers argued that since few civilians would permit them to date their daughters, why should El Pasoans complain if a trooper frequented a bar or bawdy house.

By the time congress declared war on Germany in April, 1917, soldiers and to a certain extent the politicians were at the mercy of Secretary of War Newton D. Baker who abhorred liquor and prostitution. He focused on the tiny settlement of Lynchville with its east-west boundaries being the railroad tracks and Pollard Street. Polk and Pierce streets were the north-south limits. Lynchville originated about 1912 and lasted until after the second World War, housing low-ranking military families and support businesses such as grocery stores, bars, a beer garden and a section where a few ladies of easy virtue sold and swapped their charms. Baker called for an investigation of vice in San Antonio, Laredo and El Paso—and all three communities flunked the goodness test. The secretary claimed military posts in these towns were ringed by saloons and disorderly houses. The communities could either close those places of sin, or risk losing the military posts. "El Paso must clean up," Baker thundered, "for I am in receipt of daily reports showing social conditions to which our soldiers are subjected which can no longer be tolerated."

The Ministerial Alliance of El Paso and the principal evangelical churches endorsed Baker's stand. By June, 1917, the police were raiding the red-light districts near Tenth and San Jacinto (now South Mesa) streets. This did not entirely get rid of what

Lieutenant Stacy Hinkle pilots the plane in right center as crew chief stands and salutes. This fly-by of DH-4s was part of a review for General Pershing's return to Fort Bliss after World War I. Picture was taken from where post polo field is presently located.
(Millard McKinney Collection)

the army called "hotbeds of vice," or the "festering sore" Lynchville, but the city fathers considered it a beginning.

President Woodrow Wilson placed a five-mile liquor-free zone around military camps, and soon extended it to ten miles. Lieutenant Paul Popenoe of the Army Sanitation Corps at Fort Bliss believed shady ladies were under military blankets from El Paso to Yuma, Arizona, and he vowed to "drive out every immoral woman from the vicinity of military encampments." Popenoe defined an army post as any place soldiers were stationed, including such limited areas as the camp at the Santa Fe Street Bridge.

Fort Bliss declared the streets south of Overland off-limits to military personnel. The city council made it illegal to give or sell liquor to a soldier, sailor or marine, and it routinely regulated rooming houses, bars, dance halls and hotels. The San Antonio and El Paso police departments began exchanging lists of traveling ladies who worked both towns. The *El Paso Herald* stoutly supported these reforms, but the *Times* refused to become what it called a morality zealot.

In the struggle against sin, the city fathers and the Fort Bliss sanitation people had an ally in the Kaiser, for the war in Europe attracted attention away from home. El Paso had mass parades and fiery speeches. Over three thousand local boys joined the Army, one hundred and four received wounds. Of these, sixty-three died and forty-seven won citations for bravery.

One of the outstanding heroes was Marcelino Serna, born in Chihuahua City, Mexico. General Pershing cited him. Marshal Ferdinand Foch decorated the twice-wounded Serna for capturing a machine gun and its German crew. Serna would henceforth proudly march in El Paso military parades up until the 1980s.

Major Richard F. Burges, attorney and civic leader, brought home the French Croix de Guerre for "great audacity, bravery and technical knowledge during the attack on St. Etienne á Arnes."

Hughes de Courcy Slater, editor of the *Herald*, kept a careful record of his war experiences in

France. For years afterward he shared this worldliness in his "Overseas Notebook," a special section of the *El Paso Herald*. Gradually El Pasoans began calling him "Captain" Slater.

World War I steel helmet with insignia of the Third Army. This style helmet was used by U. S. troops until early in World War II. (Fort Bliss Replica Museum)

The gallant 19th Division contained hundreds of El Paso recruits. It earned a tough reputation by holding out for seventy-five days without relief against crack German troops at St. Mihiel. None of this brought El Paso any closer to an expanded post. The Great War had nearly depleted the various units, even though the War Department stationed the 15th Provisional Cavalry Division at Fort Bliss. And as World War I faded, cantonments across the country began to shut down. Fort Bliss at least kept its doors open.

The Pershing House

QUARTERS NO. 1, "The Pershing House," was built in 1910. It is not the oldest house on Fort Bliss, but it is the most famous. The address is 228 Sheridan Road.

Colonel Alfred C. Sharpe occupied it first (1910-1911), and Major General Robert L. Howze lived in it the longest, 1919-1925.

Quarters No. 1 has been a place of memorable parties, as Brigadier General Edgar Z. Steever established its first international fame by entertaining Mexican General Victoriano Huerta in 1912. When Brigadier General Hugh Scott took over, 1913-1914, he hosted Buffalo Bill and planned regional strategy there until being relieved by Brigadier General John J. Pershing (1914-1916), for whom the house is named. During those times, Pershing entertained Pancho Villa and General Alvaro Obregón on occasion.

The house cost $16,378, an expensive home for that time. The structure was built along simple, square lines, being made of brick and having two stories as well as a full basement. Wooden covered porches extended around three sides. The building has been frequently remodeled.

The Pershing House, built in 1910, is the most famous building on post even though it was not originally constructed for General Pershing. Colorful figures such as Buffalo Bill, Pancho Villa and controversial Mexican President Victoriano Huerta have been entertained here. (Millard McKinney Collection)

In 1934 a new home was built for the commanding officer, and the Pershing House became the residence for major subordinate commanders. From 1944 through 1946 the Women's Army Corps housed its officers there. However, two Fort Bliss commanders have since chosen to live in the house: Major General John L. Homer, 1946-1950, and Major General Robert J. Lunn, 1976-1977.

The Border
Air Patrol

11

T HE UNITED STATES Air Force had its beginning on August 1, 1907 with the organization of the Aeronautical Division within the Signal Corps of the United States Army. In 1911, Congress appropriated $125,000 for training and reconnaissance, and two years later the 1st Aero Squadron took assignment at Texas City, Texas. In March, 1916, in response to Pancho Villa's raid on Columbus, New Mexico, eight JN planes of the squadron arrived by train in Columbus and assisted Pershing with the Punitive Expedition.

Due to high altitudes, low humidity, low horsepower engines, and a lack of adequate maintenance, six of the planes were grounded or wrecked within two weeks. But they had performed their mission of mail delivery and reconnaissance. Pershing praised their efforts.

Meanwhile, with Pancho Villa still running loose after the Punitive Expedition's departure from Mexico, the El Paso Southwest braced in June, 1919, for new border raids. Villa and his brilliant artillery tactician, General Felipe Angeles, brought four thousand men to the Juárez outskirts and prepared to attack.

Anticipating that fighting might carry over into El Paso, Brigadier General James B. Erwin, commander of the El Paso Military District, stationed troops along the border and in the southern part of town. Between El Paso and Ysleta he placed the 2nd Cavalry Brigade, commanded by Colonel Selah R. H. "Tommy" Tompkins, a hard-drinking, pink-whiskered, legendary veteran of the 7th Cavalry. This brigade included three squadrons of the 5th Cavalry and three squadrons of the 7th Cavalry. In addition, there was a battalion of the 82nd Field Artillery, two battalions of 8th Engineers (Mounted), a battalion of the 7th Field Signal, and one field hospital. Downtown at Florence Street, in the vicinity of 9th, 10th and 11th, Erwin stationed two battalions of the 82nd Field Artillery. Regimental headquarters of the artillery was in the El Paso Stockyards Building near the foot of Cotton Street. Two battalions of 24th Infantry, one battalion of the 19th Infantry, and one battalion of the 9th Engineers, together with Infantry Headquarters, were at the Santa Fe Street Bridge. On the mesa above El Paso High School, Erwin placed one searchlight section of the 8th Engineers.

Erwin now warned Villa and General Francisco González, Federal Commander in Juárez, that he would not tolerate firing into El Paso. If necessary he would send troops across the Rio Grande and disperse both factions.

Fort Bliss Flying Field circa 1924. Left to right, Brigadier General Walter C. Short, commander of the 2nd Cavalry Brigade and later Fort Bliss commander; Major Leo G. Heffernan, pilot and commander of Fort Bliss Flying Field; Major General Robert L. Howze, Fort Bliss commander. Note spurs on General Short. (Millard McKinney Collection)

Late at night on June 14, Villa attacked Juárez. Within hours he controlled the downtown and race track area, and had forced the Federals into defensive positions near the outskirts of town. On Sunday night, June 15, a fusillade of rifle shots struck artillery command headquarters in the El Paso Stockyards Building, killing Private Sam Tusco and seriously wounding Private Burchard Casey.

That was too much. A cussing Colonel Tommy Tompkins led the Cavalry Brigade across the Rio Grande at three fords: San Lorenzo (near where 16th of September Street presently makes its huge curve in Juárez), Senecú (across from Ascarate), and Zambrano (in the same general vicinity). One artillery caisson overturned in the Rio Grande.

Back in El Paso, snipers fired at artillery batteries A and B from tenement windows in *Chihuahuita*. A platoon of 19th Infantry rushed in and cleaned them out while the 24th Infantry advanced at midnight across the Santa Fe Street Bridge, under cover of a sixty-four round artillery barrage from El Paso aimed at the Juárez race track. Shrapnel scattered Villa's insurgents gathering in celebration.

General Erwin hoped to catch the rebels in pincers between the cavalry and the infantry, but when dawn came on Monday, most of Villa's men had escaped. An insurgent group west of Zaragoza was pounded with artillery and scattered by troopers of the 5th and 7th Cavalry.

The newspapers estimated between 100 and 200 rebel deaths. The Americans lost two men: artillery Private Sam Tusco in El Paso, and Sergeant Peter Chigas of the 7th Cavalry who died of wounds suffered in Mexico. A military site at the cement plant in El Paso would subsequently become Camp Tusco, and the camp near the Santa Fe Street Bridge would be named for Chigas.

On the morning of June 16, the 24th Infantry returned to El Paso via the downtown bridges. Late that same afternoon, the Cavalry Brigade recrossed the Rio Grande on the pontoon bridge built by the engineers near Senecú. They recovered the caisson abandoned the night before.

These border hostilities reinforced Washington's opinion that the international border would have to be more closely observed. Brigadier General William "Billy" Mitchell, Assistant Chief of the Air Service and Director of Military Aeronautics, decided that armed aerial reconnaissance could be of great assistance to cavalry patrols along the boundary. On June 16, Fort Bliss received eighteen planes, six from Kelly Field in San Antonio and twelve from Ellington Field in Houston.

The 20th Aero Squadron from Ellington consisted of twenty-nine flying officers and seventy-one enlisted men, plus a medical unit of one officer and four enlisted men. Twelve DH4 bombers dubbed "Flaming Coffins" rounded out the command. The Fort Bliss cavalry called these planes "The Big Chickens." They and the 11th Aero Squadron from Kelly Field became an important part of the Army Border Air Patrol, beginning their first reconnaissance from Fort Bliss on June 18, 1919. Their mission was to report Mexican insurgent and outlaw bands who crossed the international border into the United States.

The 12th, 96th and 104th Aero Squadrons, just returning from overseas duty, were assigned to Fort Bliss which now had five squadrons and a photographic section. These units were designated the "1st Bombardment Group," although no bombs were ever carried on patrol. On November 5, it was renamed the "1st Surveillance Group." Under the command of Major Edgar G. Tobin, World War I ace, later succeeded by Major Leo A. Walton, aerial surveillance was conducted from Nogales, Arizona to Sanderson, Texas. Fort Bliss was the headquarters. Air strips (usually pastures) were cut at Douglas, Arizona, Marfa and Sanderson, Texas. Going westward, the patrol flew along the marked border, and returned. Eastward, the patrols observed the Rio Grande to Presidio, then headed north to Marfa. After spending the night, the pilots either retraced their route back to Bliss or returned to Presidio and followed the river through the Big Bend country to Sanderson. During these flights one of the great adventures in border history occurred.

On August 10, 1919, Lieutenant Harold G. Peterson, the pilot and Paul H. Davis, the observer gunner, left Marfa for Fort Bliss. Along the way, four connecting-rod bearings in the Liberty engine burned out and forced down the DH4. The disoriented airmen thought they had been following the Rio Grande. Instead, they had been flying into Mexico along the Río Conchos—which intersects the Rio Grande at Presidio. They both survived the crash and, assuming they were in Texas, did not try to hide. Instead they started walking in a direction they hoped would bring them to a ranch house or other habitation. A few days later bandits led by Jesús Rentería captured them. Rentería demanded $15,000 ransom from the American government, or the flyers would be shot. While the United States debated what to do, Big Bend ranchers subscribed the sum. Captain Leonard F. Matlack, commanding Troop K, 8th Cavalry at Candelaria, Texas, took the money into Mexico, got both hostages out, and in the confusion of the night rescue, escaped with half the cash. With the aviators free, four columns of the 5th and 8th Cavalry penetrated into the mountain country south of the Big Bend. They captured the wrong bandits and caused an international furor when civilian scouts executed the four Mexican prisoners, an act for which Major James P. Yancey, one of the cavalry commanders, was court-martialed.

An even more unbelievable incident now happened. As the Border Air Patrol searched the badlands of Mexico, Lieutenant Frank S. Estill, encountered three horsemen who fired at him. In retaliation, Estill pointed the plane at them, that being the only way he could aim at objects on the ground, and opened fire through the propeller with the two synchronized Marlin machine guns. As the plane zoomed overhead, the observer gunner, Lieutenant Russell H. Cooper fired the twin Lewis machine guns mounted on the rear cockpit. Down went a bandit and his white horse, the rider later being identified as Jesús Rentería.

Back at Fort Bliss the airplane landing area was actually a cavalry drill field located just east of the post. At the north end stood two buildings of the former El Paso Military Institute, a private school that began operations in 1907 and went bankrupt in 1913. Within months the El Paso Chamber of Commerce purchased the property and induced the University of Texas to establish the Texas State School of Mines and Metallurgy there. It opened with twenty-seven students, most of whom rode the Fort Bliss streetcar to the end of the line—and then walked for a half-mile to the school. Except for an occasional military drill on the post, nothing broke

The 82nd Field Artillery on march through El Paso, June 16, 1919.
Troops are moving north on Campbell Street and crossing Yandell
Boulevard. Wakefield Plaza Building is at top of photo. (Millard
McKinney Collection)

the loneliness. Then in October, 1916, a fire destroyed the main building. Although study continued
in a temporary structure, the city shifted the school
to the western side of the Franklins where it is today, becoming the College of Mines and Metallurgy, then Texas Western College, and finally The
University of Texas at El Paso.

Both General Billy Mitchell and Colonel Henry
H. "Hap" Arnold (later commanding general of all
the United States Air Forces in World War II) visited Fort Bliss. They were pleased by the Border Air
Patrol's accomplishments.

And what accomplishments those were. Stacy C. Hinkle, a pilot, wrote of his exciting adventures in two engaging monographs, *Wings and Saddles* and *Wings Over the Border*. He told of outlaw sightings, of flying in unpredictable weather, of fiery crashes, of obscure landmarks, of misdirections, of unauthorized landings in Mexico, of hairbreadth escapes and unbelievable courage. He said maximum flying time for the DH4 was four hours before the plane used all its fuel. The oil was even less dependable, for it would suddenly burn out and freeze the Liberty engine. The wireless had a range of twenty-five miles, but seldom functioned. And while messages could be dropped to troops on the ground, the troops on the ground could not reply except by tediously prepared signals. He explained how the 82nd Field Artillery at Fort Bliss would haul its 75mm guns to the desert firing ranges. Since the targets were hidden from the artillerymen, the planes acted as spotters, always being careful to avoid shell trajectory and being themselves shot down.

Otherwise, the strangest craft to appear in the El Paso skies belonged to the Lighter-Than-Air Company. The Army was bringing in a twin-engine blimp from Langley Field, Virginia, and Fort Bliss began construction of a giant steel hangar on Camp Owen Beirne in late 1919, a building laid out in the wrong direction. The openings at each end should have faced the prevailing winds, west to east. Instead, the hangar was built in a north-south direction, and the winds sometimes knocked the gas bag sideways when it was taken in or out. As gusts often rocked Camp Beirne, the blimp usually stayed in the hanger. The 8th Balloon Company, later the 8th Airship Company, did make several flights over the

Eighth Airship Company dirigible entering the hangar at Fort Bliss Balloon Field in 1922. A landmark for many years, the hangar was dismantled in 1955. (El Paso Public Library)

El Paso neighborhood, but was never assigned to border patrol duty, as was originally intended.

During 1920 the first parachute arrived, and Lieutenant Ulrick Bouquet volunteered to see how it worked. He jumped from an altitude of about fifteen hundred feet on a windless day in April. Not having any experience, Bouquet plunged head first when he left the plane, counted three and jerked the cord. He said later that the chute opening "damned near snapped my boots off." Nevertheless, the lieutenant landed solidly but alive on the flying field.

By early 1921, with General Billy Mitchell predicting that airplanes could sink a battleship, the Army began bombing tests at several Air Service stations, including Camp Beirne. Stacy Hinkle and other pilots practiced with 25, 50 and 100 pound bombs on the cavalry target range. On May 11, instructor Captain Lloyd Harvey, and lieutenants Stacy C. Hinkle, Leo F. Post, Edgar A. Liebhauser and Dale V. Gaffney left Fort Bliss for Kelly Field in San Antonio. From there the officers went by train to Langley Field where they participated during June and July in sinking four German warships turned over to the United States after World War I.

During June, orders arrived to terminate the Border Air Patrol. The 8th Airship Company was transferred from Camp Beirne to Brooks Field, San Antonio. With the exception of Fort Bliss, all military airfields were closed along the Mexican border. The six remaining planes at Bliss were assigned to the 1st Cavalry Division. With this change in command, aviators at Fort Bliss were required to wear Division insignia patches on their uniform jacket and, of more distress to the pilots, they also had to wear spurs.

Captain Claire L. Chennault, the aviation engineer officer of the 12th Aero Squadron served at the Fort Bliss Air Terminal from 1922 to 1924. Later in World War II, he commanded the "Flying Tigers" and the 14th Air Force in China.

Meanwhile, on January 5, 1925, the Fort Bliss Air Terminal was named Biggs Field in honor of Lieutenant James B. "Buster" Biggs. As an El Paso aviator, he had died in a plane crash at Beltrain, France in October, 1918. Within a few years Biggs would become a significant military part of the El Paso Southwest.

William Beaumont Army Medical Center

12

WILLIAM BEAUMONT Army Medical Center is the fifth military hospital for Fort Bliss, although it could be the sixth if the hospital at Camp Concordia is counted. That building was a former residence (perhaps the old Hugh Stephenson hacienda), a structure located off the military reservation.

Otherwise, the first hospital was at Hart's Mill. Patients suffered primarily from ailments traced to the unpurified Rio Grande water. When Fort Bliss moved to Lanoria Mesa in 1893, what is now Building 8 became the hospital. The primary medical facility shifted to Building 1 in 1916, but it has been at the William Beaumont site ever since.

The twelve-story William Beaumont Medical Center nestles on the desert floor below Sugarloaf Peak in the Franklin Mountains. (Millard McKinney Collection)

The present hospital is named for a man far removed from the El Paso Southwest. Dr. William Beaumont joined the 6th Infantry as an assistant surgeon, and saw action during the War of 1812. In 1820 he accepted assignment at Fort Mackinac, Michigan, where his experiments and observations would make him famous in years to come.

A brawny, eighteen-year-old French Canadian fur trapper named Alexis St. Martin was shot at close range with a musket in 1822. The charge blew away much of his stomach and chest, exposing portions of his intestines, lungs and ribs. Beaumont arrived within minutes, dressed the wounds and waited for him to die. Instead, the patient lived to be eighty-three, and fathered twenty children.

St. Martin's wound never healed, and Dr. Beaumont thus had a window into the intestines from which to take body temperatures and observe the intricate and mysterious stomach processes. Beaumont's careful notes and observations revolutionized medical understanding of how the organs functioned. When the physician closed out his brilliant, twenty-five year Army career, dying in 1853, he had numerous honors. On June 26, 1920, the Army paid its ultimate respect by starting construction of William Beaumont General Hospital in El Paso.

Work began on 272 acres of rocky, cactus-covered land northwest of Fort Bliss proper, an area now roughly encompassed by Dyer Street and Piedras, Hayes Street and Fred Wilson Road. Rattlesnakes infested the steep arroyos. Today the atmosphere is quiet and relaxed, the grounds having grass, flowers, shrubs and trees.

The tile and stucco buildings cost several million dollars and opened on July 1, 1921 with a bed capacity of 403 patients. The staff numbered six medical officers, two nurses and thirty enlisted men.

Beaumont underwent little expansion until World War II when it grew into 174 buildings and a crowded 4,064 beds. (These included the 1,000 beds at the Fort Bliss Station Hospital and the 750 beds at Biggs Field.) During early 1945, approximately 6,000 patients were treated. Additional staff quarters multiplied at Pierce and Hayes streets, and at Justus and Piedras. A military school for medical technicians offered specialized training in surgical, dental, laboratory, X-ray, pharmacy and veterinary techniques. The hospital had a fully-equipped physical therapy and occupational therapy center. An artificial eye clinic opened. Beaumont expanded into an outstanding hospital for neuropsychiatric treatment and orthopedic surgery.

One of its best accomplishments was the plastic surgery center, established in December, 1943. The first chief of plastic surgery was Lieut. Colonel Willard W. Schuessler, who would become one of the foremost plastic surgeons in El Paso. Dr. Schuessler was appointed civilian aide to the Secretary of the Army in 1980, succeeding William I. Latham, retired editor of *The El Paso Times*. The surgeon's rise to civilian aide was a distinction rarely accorded physicians.

Major General Charles G. Pixley, the hospital commander from September, 1975 through 1976 also achieved high eminence. Dr. Pixley was given his third star in 1977 and became Surgeon General of the Army with offices in the Pentagon.

As Fort Bliss continued to expand during the next two decades, William Beaumont outran its capabilities. The alternative was a new hospital by the same name, one built alongside and to the west of the old facilities, and dedicated on July 1, 1972.

Twelve stories reached above the desert floor, an eight-level tower protruding from a massive four-story base. The building's façade of cream-colored brick and sandblasted natural concrete blended with the Franklin Mountains, a half-mile west. The base covered an area in excess of two acres, the twelve levels containing more than a half-million square feet of floor space. By the early 1980s, the hospital had a capacity of 463, although it was designed for 611. Since then the structure has become so imposing that when one drives Route 45 north from Chihuahua City, Mexico, the Beaumont Hospital tower is the first building to appear in El Paso as the traveler nears Juárez from the south.

On April 1, 1973, the hospital became the bedrock for a vast three-state government medical complex known as William Beaumont Army Medical Center, the cornerstone of Health Service Region No. 4. It includes Texas west of the Pecos River, New Mexico and Arizona. Six Air Force bases and three Army posts (including Fort Bliss) are a part. Beaumont is the chief medical facility for White Sands Missile Range, the Mescalero and Zuni Indians, plus the La Tuna Federal Prison near Anthony, New Mexico-Texas. While Beaumont ministers to active duty personnel, dependents and retired military people, it will treat civilians too on an emergency basis.

Virtually every medical and surgical specialty and sub-specialty is practiced at the hospital. A heliport is available alongside the emergency room entrance for patients arriving by air ambulance.

Beaumont also has an exclusive function—a trauma unit. It provides resuscitation, treatment and rehabilitation of the seriously ill or injured patient. Furthermore, it conducts investigations into the causes and treatment of trauma—its findings being made known through publishing programs and the training of outside people.

The $2.7 million Troop Medical and Dental Clinic at Fort Bliss has taken much of the strain off the main hospital medical staff. Its treatment facilities handle ailments not ordinarily requiring hospital care.

During the early 1980s, William Beaumont Army Medical Center and its clinics would examine an estimated 900,000 outpatients, hospitalize 18,500 people, conduct 13 million laboratory examinations, process over 650,000 film exposures, and deliver nearly 2,000 babies. Its budget would run about $28 million, including salaries for approximately 1,000 civilians and 1,000 military.

Construction of the General of the Army Omar M. Bradley Building began on March 31, 1980, on the west side of the hospital tower. At a cost of $13 million, the annex would add 120,000 square feet to the hospital in addition to consolidating outpatient and administrative services.

The hospital is a tenant of Fort Bliss, subordinate to Health Services Command which supervises seven health service regions in the United States. Its headquarters are at Fort Sam Houston, Texas.

The Horse Cavalry

13

N O UNIT CAN MATCH the impact upon Fort Bliss as did the 1st Cavalry Division. It was activated during 1921-22, and became a legend not only for its heroic accomplishments, especially during World War II, but because of the regiments and battalions that comprised it.

The 1st Cavalry Regiment was organized March 4, 1833 as the U.S. Regiment of Dragoons, and then was redesignated on August 3, 1861 as the 1st Cavalry. It participated in the Mexican War, the Indian Wars, the Civil War, the War with Spain and the Philippine Insurrection. Assigned to Mexican Border duty, with headquarters at Douglas, Arizona prior to the First World War, the regiment joined the 1st Cavalry Division on August 20, 1921. On January 3, 1933 while stationed at Marfa, Texas the regiment was transferred to Fort Knox, Kentucky where it was reorganized and redesignated as 1st Cavalry, Mechanized.

In 1855 the 5th Cavalry Regiment was organized, taking part in forty engagements against the Indians before the Civil War. Lieut. Colonel Robert E. Lee was in command of the 5th when he resigned from the Union Army, and was then selected by the South to lead their armies against those of the North. Subsequent to the Civil War the 5th engaged in ninety-four more battles with various Indian tribes. It saw action in Puerto Rico during the Spanish-American War and in the Philippines during the Insurrection of 1901. It returned to the United States in 1903, spent five years on the western frontier and then served in the Hawaiian Department for four years. After returning to the States, the regiment spent eleven months with Pershing's Expedition in Mexico before being assigned to Fort Bliss and border patrol duty.

The 7th Cavalry Regiment is the best known of all, and its story is told elsewhere in this book. It and the 8th Cavalry Regiment would be the most closely identified with Fort Bliss.

Right after the Civil War, the 8th Cavalry Regiment was created, and for the next few years fought Indians from Oregon to New Mexico. Its record of one hundred fifty hostile engagements is nearly unequaled in frontier infantry or cavalry history. The 8th fought in Cuba once, and in the Philippines twice. It patrolled the Mexican border in the Big Bend country during 1915, on nineteen different occasions riding shotgun for the Southern Pacific because the railroad believed itself menaced by Mexican bandits and American desperados.

The 82nd Field Artillery was established during

The yellow and black shoulder sleeve insignia of the 1st Cavalry Division was designed by Mrs. Ben H. Dorcy of Fort Bliss. (Millard McKinney Collection)

the First World War at Fort D. A. Russell, Wyoming when the 24th Cavalry was reorganized into a horse artillery unit. Although the newly designated artillerymen were given a full complement of horses and mules, field guns were not assigned. Therefore, in order to conduct training, the men improvised artillery carriages and "dummy" guns from surplus material that was rustled on the post. The regiment, still without real artillery equipment, was transferred to Camp Logan, Texas in November 1917 and then to Fort Bliss the following month. The first real guns were received in March 1918. The 82nd Field Artillery became a unit of the 1st Cavalry Division in September 1921.

Another fighting outfit that took its place in the Division was the 12th Cavalry regiment, although it was comparatively young as an organization. Activated in 1901, it had been to the Philippines, and had served in Nebraska, Arizona and the Dakotas. It had restored order in the Colorado strike zone. Pershing's supply trains relied heavily on Troop H for support during the Punitive Expedition.

The 8th Engineer Battalion (Mounted) was organized by verbal order of General Pershing on August 20, 1916 at Twin Windmills, Mexico during the Punitive Expedition.

Other units serving with the 1st Cavalry Division prior to 1941, were Ambulance Company No. 43, the 61st Artillery Battalion, the 62nd Field Artillery Battalion, the 16th Quartermaster Squadron, the 1st Medical Squadron, the 1st Signal Troop (which strung military telegraph wire around the Southwest), the 27th Ordnance Company, the Tank Pursuit Squadron, the Headquarters Troop of the 1st and 2nd Brigades.

By 1941, the 1st Cavalry Division could field over ten thousand soldiers.

In order to maintain preparedness, the Division started maneuvers in 1923 at Marfa, Texas. There were many subsequent maneuvers, one of the more impressive happening in April, 1936 when a military game proved the efficient and indispensable use of cavalry. Near Camp Marfa, Brigadier General Hamilton S. Hawkins, Division Commander, demonstrated that if the Germans had exploited their cavalry in a more effective manner during World War I, they could have turned the tide of battle a few times. Not only did an impressive group of Washington brass watch the maneuvers, but so did Brigadier General Vladimer A. Burzin, the Soviet attaché.

In 1948 during its annual reunion, the 1st Cavalry Division Association awarded a plaque and honorary membership to General Jonathan Wainwright, the hero of Corregidor. Major General William C.

Chase, commander of the 1st Cavalry Division in Japan, made the presentation during ceremonies at El Paso's Liberty Hall. Wainwright brought the 1st Cavalry Brigade from Fort Clark, Texas, for maneuvers in 1939. He spent the entire trip in the saddle.

During the period of 1st Cavalry Division build-up, a series of land purchases and acquisitions began at Fort Bliss. The first of these started in 1919, and was known as the Border Project. The Army constructed a group of storehouses at Fort Bliss, enabling the post to give up twenty-five large buildings rented for storage purposes in El Paso. When Brigadier General Joseph G. Castner took command in 1926, he increased the reservation by 1,059 acres, an extension which included the new Biggs Army Air Field, formerly on leased land. He also arranged the purchase of what is now Castner Range, approximately 3,272 acres at a cost of $40,640.

Negotiations faltered for the next few years as Fort Bliss occasionally acquired bits of federally-owned land such as a banco, a piece of territory tucked inside a horseshoe curve of the Rio Grande at Socorro, Texas. The State Department transferred all 270 acres of the banco to Fort Bliss because the Division needed it for maneuvers difficult to perform on the mesa.

A second expansion program began in 1934, a program designed as much to relieve the Depression as to enlarge the post. The government built thirty-eight new officers' homes, all of Spanish-style architecture with tile roofs, three bathrooms, sleeping porch, basement, garage and landscaped lawns. Five enlisted barracks were constructed, these having linoleum-covered floors, and reading rooms. New roads were constructed on post, and old ones repaired. The south theater was converted into a non-sectarian chapel. Nevertheless, in spite of a 46,000 acre Dona Ana Range across the Texas line in New Mexico, the Division had insufficient room to practice maneuvers. Areas around Marfa and Balmorhea, Texas, were utilized for these.

With the arrival of the 1940s, and war edging closer to the North American continent, Fort Bliss started an aggressive campaign to purchase additional land. It filed a friendly condemnation suit against the Texas College of Mines and picked up twenty-two acres of property owned by the school in the center of the post. The Army also sued to obtain the old ghost town of Tobin near present Sunrise Shopping Center. Frank R. Tobin, a real estate developer, proposed this townsite in 1907, and had sold hundreds of lots. By 1940 almost none of the owners could be found. Roughly the same situation existed at Logan Heights, a future site for intensive recruit training, and a Separation Center for World War II veterans. The El Paso Chamber of Commerce attempted without success to purchase all 1,027 acres, but most owners refused to sell. So the Army condemned the land for national defense in October, and constructed barracks for 12,024 enlisted men and 574 officers.

In an unprecedented action, the city council and commissioners court authorized the Army to take possession of 1,800 acres near the Baptist Sanitarium, now the Spanish Baptist Publishing House. More than a hundred owners could not be located, and the resolution passed within an hour's notice during an emergency meeting.

Fort Bliss now had a remarkable territorial area comprising roughly 404,000 acres or 630 square miles. It included the 5,000 acre post reservation,

First Cavalry Division troops trail down the east side of El Paso's rugged Scenic Drive in mid-1920s. The drive was built with chain gang labor. (Millard McKinney Collection)

52,000 acres adjoining it to the east and northeast, the Castner Target Range of 3,272 acres, the Dona Ana Target Range of 46,000 acres, and another 350,000 acres of New Mexico land leased for an anti-aircraft range. For spring maneuvers, Bliss had trespass rights on an additional 200,000 acres of New Mexico property. Thus the post in 1940 either owned or leased all of the desert between the Organ and Hueco Mountains (about fifty miles apart), and from Fort Bliss proper to near White Sands National Monument on the north.

But early 1940 and 1941 was still the time of the horse. As late as March, 1941, the army bought 1,052 horses for the post, a figure raising the total horse population to 8,000. Most were geldings, as stallions tended to fight, and mares kicked the troopers.

Horse shows were popular, and as there were no civilian opportunities in town, El Pasoans took their animals to Bliss. Regiments participated from as far away as Brownsville. During the spring and fall, competitors put their favorite mounts through jumping and riding events usually at Howze Stadium, a site between the officers quarters on Sheridan Road and the enlisted barracks on Pershing Road. Two concrete jumps are still there.

Polo games began during the early 1900s and to a limited extent still occur. There were inter-divisional matches, a lot of stiff regimental competition, matches with civilian players from El Paso, and matches with Juárez teams. At least five fields existed at one time or another on Fort Bliss, and every regiment had its practice area. All permanent sites were of hard-packed sand, although several were later sodded. The fields originally had regimental designations, but the practice grew that when a

The last of the horse soldiers played out their roles at Fort Bliss in the early 1940s. These troopers maneuver on the escarpment north of present-day I-10, between what is now Yarbrough and Lomaland drives. (Frank Mangan Collection)

man was killed while playing, a field would be named in his memory. There was Bosserman Field, west of the post cemetery for Lieutenant Raymond Bosserman. Noel Field, for Lieutenant Paul Noel, was between Sheridan and Pershing roads, west of the Fort Bliss Replica, Armstrong Field, for Lieutenant Eugene Armstrong, was and is the site west of the present Officer's Club. Armstrong was on detached duty from the 13th Cavalry in Columbus, New Mexico, when he was killed while playing polo in Washington Park.

Army campaign hat was standard issue until early in World War II. (Frank Mangan)

Shows during the Southwestern Open Polo Tournaments attracted thousands of spectators, Howze Stadium usually being filled to overflowing. The 7th and 8th Cavalry Regiments generally fielded the best teams, the 7th in particular being a constant Southwestern champion and a national contender. The post teams dueled with top military talent as well as highly-rated teams from Mexico City, and often won.

Fort Bliss treated its horses well. Light horses got a field ration containing nine pounds of oats and nineteen pounds of hay daily, whereas heavier horses (over 1,150 pounds) received eleven pounds of oats and twenty-two pounds of hay. Each horse received one daily ounce of salt. When ill, the animals went to the Fort Bliss veterinary hospital with its medical facilities for ten thousand horses. The resources included a pharmacy, operating tables, skilled surgeons, dental experts, anesthesiologists — everything in fact except pretty nurses. If the horse did not respond, it was shot. The Army refused to pension horses no longer of value. They were not auctioned, so they never spent their old age in the Juárez bullring or in pulling a banana cart.

Garry Owen was the most famous mount of all, being named after an old Irish drinking song which was also the theme music for the 7th Cavalry. Garry Owen Drive in El Paso memorializes this horse. In 1928 he scored his greatest triumph by winning twenty-eight jumping and running events at Madison Square Garden. The big gray was ridden to victory more times than any other mount in the history of the United States Army. When fifteen years old, a cavalry horse kicked him in the leg, breaking a bone, and Garry Owen's brilliant career ended with a bullet in his head. The location of his grave is not presently known, although a gravestone commemorates him in the Pet Cemetery of the Fort Bliss Replica Museum. The stones would have one believe that Garry Owen sleeps beside "Our Pal," "Lady," "Miss McClure," and "Buddy," when actually there are no horses buried there at all. The names are of famous mounts that the Army wishes to remember.

In June, 1943, the Army phased out the horse cavalry. The 1st Cavalry Division, now completely dismounted and mechanized, headed for the South Pacific.

The horse soldiers had never totally dominated the post anyway. Mechanized units arrived at Fort Bliss in 1928. On November 8, three light armored cars, eight medium armored cars, two motorcycles and two trucks reached Fort Bliss from the East Coast. It was the first experiment of the United States Army mechanized units. Known as the 1st Armored Car Troop, it was attached to the 1st Cavalry Division and stationed in the old Engineers barracks in the artillery area. The public swarmed out to see the new machines, but considered them an interesting novelty, feeling certain they would never replace the horse.

The 7th Cavalry

No REGIMENT equals the 7th Cavalry Regiment in legendary exploits. Lieut. Colonel George Armstrong Custer, its most famous and controversial commander, joined at its inception at Fort Riley, Kansas, in 1866. During 1868 the 7th fought the Battle of Washita, slaying the Cheyenne chief, Black Kettle.

Eight years later the winners were reversed at the Little Big Horn in Montana. Custer and 265 men were wiped out in 1876 by Sioux and Cheyenne warriors.

The 7th regrouped, and in 1890 participated in the Battle of Wounded Knee, South Dakota, losing twenty-five soldiers. Not long afterwards, elements of the 7th patrolled the Mexican border from forts Hancock, Sam Houston and Clark, all in Texas.

By the middle and late 1890s, the 7th occupied Fort Bayard, New Mexico and forts Apache, Huachuca and Grant, in Arizona. The 7th ceaselessly searched for the Apache Kid and his band of renegade Indians along the Mexican border. Units in hot pursuit occasionally penetrated into Sonora, Mexico.

After serving valiantly in Cuba, the 7th went twice to the Philippines, returning to the Southwest and to Douglas, Arizona in 1915. General Pershing attached them to his Mexican Punitive Expedition in 1916. When the 7th left Mexico, it marched to Fort Bliss and assumed duties along the Rio Grande between Ysleta and Fabens, Texas.

On June 15, 1919, most of the regiment crossed the Rio Grande in pursuit of Pancho Villa. After scattering the Villistas in Juárez and again in Zaragoza, the military returned home.

For the next few years the 7th performed garrison duties at Fort Bliss, patrolling the river, guarding the bridges, and making extended marches to Cloudcroft and Elephant Butte Dam, New Mexico, as well as to Marfa, Texas. By 1921, the 7th had become part of the 1st Cavalry Division at Fort Bliss. Although the unit saw no action for the next two decades, the 1929 Escobar revolt in Mexico caused a general tightening of border security along the Rio Grande.

In February, 1943, the War Department dismounted the 1st Cavalry Division, and hence the 7th Cavalry Regiment.

14 Biggs: the Wild Blue Yonder

THE FIRST BIGGS FIELD began in June 1919 with headquarters at the old School of Mines dormitory on the east side of Fort Bliss—now in the center of the main post complex. When that field closed in July, 1926, the designation was transferred to the former balloon field located a mile to the northeast. The balloon field had already acquired three hangars, achieving sufficient regional importance that it later became Biggs Air Force Base. Its namesake had been Lieutenant James B. "Buster" Biggs.

Although Biggs served mostly transient aircraft, it also catered to transcontinental travelers, one being the renowned aviator Charles A. Lindbergh. Shortly after his historic transatlantic flight, Lindbergh started a tour of American cities, landing at Biggs on September 24, 1927 amid a "din of auto horns." A parade took him to the El Paso High School Stadium where he urged El Pasoans to strive for a city airport. William J. "Bill" Hooten, a reporter for the *El Paso Herald* (and eventually editor of *The El Paso Times*), wrote in his *Fifty-Two Years a Newsman*, that Lindbergh learned belatedly of a scheduled visit to the disabled veterans at William Beaumont Army Hospital. Hooten said Lindbergh went later to the hospital and strolled through the wards, saying repeatedly, "Boys, I would not have passed you up for anything."

Following the demise of the Border Air Patrol, one officer, twelve airmen and one plane kept Biggs Field alive until 1939. Its 208 acres of land included one balloon hangar and two aircraft hangars. Radio control towers were added in 1939, along with a restaurant and maintenance shop.

The 20th Observation Squadron and a Tow Target Squadron arrived in 1939 also. The 0-47s towed sleeve targets for the 260th Coast Artillery Regiment. Sometimes during these exercises, things went wrong as in October, 1941, when a plane approached low over the San Andres Mountains and attempted a "surprise attack." Instead the plane struck a hillside at Ash Canyon, thirty-five miles northeast of Las Cruces, New Mexico. All three crew members died.

A $10 million construction program in 1941 expanded Biggs Army Air Field into a modern air base. The 2nd Air Force moved into Biggs a year later and assumed command of all heavy bombardment training in the United States. The 20th Bombardment Command with its B-17 Flying Fortresses and B-24 Liberator bombers brought its headquarters to Biggs. Army Air Force personnel and warplanes began arriving in increasing waves as Biggs cranked up heavily for the Second World War effort. Bombers being ferried to England during the Battle of Britain roared daily over El Paso, and were serviced at Biggs.

The luck of more than a few airmen ran out. On a cool night in late March, 1944, a B-24 left Biggs on a routine flight, and crashed into Red Rock Canyon near the painted "A" representing Austin High School. Seven crew members were killed on that eastern slope of Mt. Franklin. Marcos Uribe, a janitor at the El Paso Public Library, watched the crash and explosion from his home, and thought how tragic it was that he should be so safe and secure while other men were dying. (Uribe was born in Coahuila, Mexico, and became a United States citizen in 1943.) Acting substantially alone, but with the assistance and prayers of parishioners of Our Lady of Guadalupe Church on Alabama Street, and its pastor, Father Raymundo García, he erected a temporary concrete cross at the crash site. Today a more permanent fixture stands at remote Red Rock Canyon, a fifteen-foot cross of wood and sheet metal set in a concrete base, a monument to man's compassion for man.

By 1945 the runways at Biggs were extended five hundred feet to accommodate B-29 aircraft. Fort Bliss contributed additional land, and Biggs Army Air Field grew to nearly four thousand acres. Hundreds of bomber crews practiced on an around-the-clock basis.

Biggs Field became headquarters for the 16th Bombardment Operational Training Wing, a wing that deactivated when World War II ended. The 19th Tactical Air Command, the 20th Fighter Group, and the 471st Air Service Group moved in to fill the vacuum. In December, 1946, the 19th Air

Force transferred its headquarters to Biggs from Greenville, South Carolina. The 47th Bomb Group and the 544th Air Service Group came to Biggs, as did the 12th Air Force, although its headquarters remained at March Field, California. Runways were lengthened again in 1947.

In 1947, the United States Army relinquished its command over the skies. Biggs Army Air Field officially became Biggs Air Force Base.

Three months later the 97th Bombardment Wing left Smokey Hill (now Schilling) Air Force Base in Kansas to become the primary unit at Biggs, although it served under the 8th Air Force. By now Biggs had a serious housing need, so Fort Bliss contributed additional land south of the base for an eight hundred unit development called Aero Vista. It lies between Fred Wilson Road and the El Paso International Airport.

As Biggs was an important segment of the Strategic Air Command, the bombardment wings came and went, were organized and were deactivated. The B-29s were phased out by the B-50s, and these in turn were forced into retirement by the B-36. The B-36s, giant bombers with six propellers pushing from the trailing edge of the wing, thundered into Biggs during the early 1950s. Portions of one still remain on the west side of the Franklin Mountains, the victim of a cold, snowy day when it failed to clear the rim as it groped toward Biggs for a landing.

The last B-36 left Biggs in 1959 for Amon Carter Airport at Fort Worth where it became a permanent museum piece for this particular model.

The B-36 shared its space with the B-47, a jet bomber initially using the El Paso International Airport because of better landing facilities. On a cold evening in March, 1954, as the wind gusted sand and debris into the thickening sky, a B-47 on a survey flight, circling for a landing, clipped a telephone pole at Chelsea and Montana streets, and pancaked into a vacant area staked out for new houses near Chelsea and Trowbridge streets. It struck alongside a home at 1605 Passero recently purchased by television personality Jack Rye. Flaming debris set the building afire. The three-man crew perished.

With the retirement of the B-36 and the B-47, eight B-52 Strato-Fortresses reached Biggs in late 1959 and became part of the 95th Bombardment Wing. These were closely followed by aerial refuelers, the KC-135s. With these eight-jet-engine bombers, no part of the world was too remote for their vengeance.

The *Ciudad Juárez* was the second B-52 to land at Biggs—and twenty thousand onlookers cheered as it and two others flew in formation over the base. After it parked, Mrs. René Mascarenas, wife of the mayor of Juárez, christened the *Ciudad Juárez* while her husband symbolically accepted the aircraft for his community. However, the applause soon turned to tears. As it carried out a training mission on April 7, 1961, a Sidewinder missile jarred loose from a National Guard aircraft and homed in on a heat-producing jet engine of the *Ciudad Juárez*, shooting it down. Three crew members died; four others bailed out.

With the B-52s, the most advanced bomber ever stationed at Biggs Air Force Base, the mission of the field crested. World War II had given Biggs its reason for existence and growth. Now the airfield was a victim of the success it helped create. Just as communication and transportation had shrunk the

An Air Force guard stands by a C-141 transport as a B-52H taxies toward take off. These planes were deployed to Biggs Army Air Field during a bombing exercise in June 1981. (Joel Salcido, El Paso Times)

West and spelled the demise of the small, isolated army posts, so the gigantic airplane with its mid-air refueling capabilities had made the world just a bit more tiny. Biggs could be closed at no sacrifice of national security. In 1965, the KC-135s were transferred to Dyess Air Force Base, Texas. The 431st Air Refueling Squadron was deactivated. The number of personnel at Biggs dwindled.

By middle February, 1966, it was all over. *El Paso Times* editor William I. "Bill" Latham climbed aboard the last B-52 at Biggs, the *Ciudad Juárez II*, and flew to Tucson, Arizona. Biggs Air Force Base was deactivated, to be reclaimed by Fort Bliss.

While the field still maintains transient aircraft facilities, it has become home for several training groups. Two of these are the Defense Logistical Agency and the Nuclear Bacteriological and Chemical Defense School.

Best known of all the schools is the United States Army Sergeants Major Academy, created on July 1, 1972. It is the senior level of the noncommissioned officer education system. It includes also a limited number of highly-qualified non-coms from the Air Force, Navy and Marine Corps. Subjects cover a broad range of professionalism, world affairs, management, organization and operations. Those noncommissioned officers chosen are considered some of the best soldiers in the world. Selections are made at no less a level than the Department of the Army. The twenty-two week course is held twice annually.

A similar school at Biggs is the United States Army Noncommissioned Officers Academy. Its subject material is slightly more basic than that offered the Sergeants Major. However, the quality of graduates is no less exceptional.

As for the airfield, the base has come practically full circle in terms of name. It is once again Biggs Army Air Field.

The Rockets
Red Glare:
White Sands

ROCKETS HAVE ALWAYS held the world's imagination. They open skylights into heaven; and they have the practical benefit of strengthening national defense.

Most Americans assume the U.S. missile program started when the Army grabbed 118 German rocketmen during the end of World War II. Actually the program was well underway in 1943 with a government contract for missile development with the California Institute of Technology. The Institute combined with Army Ordnance to form ORDCIT.

By late 1944, ORDCIT had vehicles ready for testing, and no place to go. The Army had been trying to acquire additional land in New Mexico alongside the Fort Bliss firing ranges, property acquisitions then incomplete. As a result, ORDCIT chose the Camp Irwin Reservation in California's Mojave Desert, and commenced firing short range test missiles known as "Private A's." These were tests to determine propulsion, aerodynamics, fin control surfaces, and to a certain extent the response to meteorological conditions.

With ORDCIT now ready for bigger things, it moved to the Tularosa Basin in early 1945. It would occupy the Bliss antiaircraft ranges, specifically the Hueco, Dona Ana, Orogrande and Alamogordo Bombing Range. By April, ORDCIT was firing what it called "Private F's," a modification of the California missiles.

As ORDCIT's test led it toward the Corporal, a sophisticated, long-range artillery missile, other events crucially came to the fore. The Army had not only captured numerous German missile experts, it had acquired carloads of V-2 parts for shipment to the United States. The government had furthermore signed a contract with Bell Telephone Laboratories for the Nike series of antiaircraft guided missiles.

By late 1944 a team of experts was evaluating various national test sites. It initially considered a location near El Centro, California. The State Department hoped to work out an agreement with Mexico and fire missiles over its territory. When international complications made that unfeasible, hawk-nosed Lieut. Colonel Harold R. Turner, a leader of the team and a man who would become the first White Sands commander, convinced his associates of New Mexico's virtues, namely the Tularosa Basin between the Sacramento Mountains on the east and the San Andres and Organ Mountains on the west. It was a land of moderate climate, nearly unlimited visibility, and sparse population. Spent missiles

Ten seconds after detonation. The world's first atomic bomb, dubbed "Fat Man," was exploded on July 16, 1945, at Trinity Site in the north-central part of the range. (White Sands Missile Range)

could easily be recovered, the possibilities of civilian injuries and civilian prying eyes, lessened.

Fort Bliss already owned much of the property, and it took no remarkable insight to see how two government agencies might be inexorably linked. The missile range would perform research, testing and development. Fort Bliss could train soldiers in operation and performance.

White Sands Proving Ground was established on July 9, 1945, effectively taking over the lands occupied by ORDCIT and effectively absorbing its mission. It also absorbed, and took the name of, the White Sands National Monument whose boundaries are inside the missile range, but controlled and operated by the National Park Service. A week after dedication, the world's first atomic bomb, dubbed "Fat Man," was exploded at Trinity Site in the north-central part of the range.

But there were "misunderstandings" in these early days, some of them "in-house." ORDCIT and White Sands had taken control of the former Fort Bliss firing ranges, a fact not pleasing to the Army at Bliss in spite of its needs for artillery practice being met. The same arrangement applied to the Army Air Corps with regard to the Alamogordo Bombing Range.

Fort Bliss stubbornly tried to retain control. As late as 1947 and 1948, soldiers frequently moved unannounced onto the Orogrande firing range. If the missile men happened to be using the facility, the Army blithely fired right over their heads. In a fit of pique, Fort Bliss even closed the War Highway from El Paso to White Sands and forced innumerable El Pasoans into relocating their residences to Las Cruces, New Mexico, which had the only other route into the missile base. Although White Sands began immediate construction of a road linking the complex headquarters with Orogrande, New Mexico, on U.S. Highway 54 (and made it more convenient for El Pasoans to reach the base), the road arrived too late to prevent the exodus to Las Cruces.

Even after the controversy was finally resolved, and White Sands had indisputable command of the firing ranges, occasional problems still persisted. Without notification, Fort Bliss would frequently close the El Paso-White Sands road for short periods due to Army firing schedules. However, most White Sands personnel were charitable enough to regard these as communications errors, rather than harassment.

Similar difficulties subsequently arose between the Alamogordo Army Air Field and White Sands. The air base had originally been built to British specifications, which explains its unusual layout. The English had anticipated B-24 practices on the nearby Alamogordo Bombing Range. When that did not materialize, the Americans utilized the base and the range themselves. This almost caused a burp in world history when a B-29, during a night bombing run, had navigational errors and dropped its load near the atomic bomb being prepared for detonation. Fortunately, nobody was hurt, and very little was damaged. Then in 1947, when the Department of Defense replaced the War Department, and the Air Force divorced the Army and decided to live on its own, the Air Force tried to assume control over Alamogordo Air Base as well as the bombing range. The Air Force began firing its own missiles not only without asking permission of White Sands but without even notifying the missile base. It was not

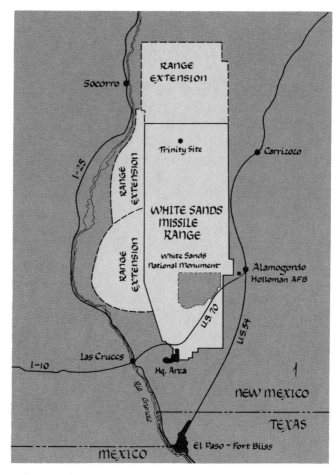

White Sands Missile Range sprawls over a vast area of southern New Mexico's Tularosa Basin. (Placido Cano)

until 1952 that a Defense Department directive firmly established the bombing range command at White Sands.

On February 17, 1948, Alamogordo Air Force Base became Holloman Air Force Base. Holloman is today an integral part of the White Sands complex because of its ability to fire air-to-air and air-to-ground missiles. It also has lesser known but extremely important capabilities, one of these being a track originally built for the SNARK, an air-breathing, winged, non-piloted airborne torpedo designed to move by rocket sled down a track until being catapulted into the sky. The project was eventually transferred to Cape Canaveral and phased out. During the 1950s, Colonel John Stapp made history at Holloman with twenty-nine sled rides on that same rocket track, experiments testing man's ability to withstand G forces at supersonic speeds. Nowadays the track tests ejection seats for fighter planes and space shuttles, and it conducts experiments as to what might happen should a space vehicle or warhead encounter violent thunderstorms upon reentry into the earth's atmosphere.

Meanwhile, German scientists had been quartered at the Ordnance Research and Development Center at Fort Bliss, being shuttled back and forth to White Sands as the Americans began firing the Tiny Tim sounding rocket and the WAC Corporal rocket.

But on April 16, 1946, the missile genius Dr. Wernher von Braun watched as the first American-based V-2 grunted, belched fire, inched off the launching pad, hovered, then lurched into the sky. Two years later specialists hitched the WAC Corporal to the nose of a V-2, and thus was created the first two-stage missile, the Bumper.

In 1958 White Sands Proving Ground changed its name to the White Sands Missile Range.

Yet as these missiles reached further into space, the German and American rocketmen scoring more and more successes, needed more and more land —

and this meant displacing people. Public hearings took place in Las Cruces, New Mexico, the government patiently explaining how it needed additional property to protect the liberty of those who were being displaced. The independent, tobacco-chewing cowmen had spent lifetimes battling blizzards, drought, Indians, big outfits and sheepherders. These ranchers had stood alone against the world, never asking for assistance, fearing only the banker and possibly God. They were a quiet, law-abiding bunch who, in the twilight of their lives, with some notable exceptions, possessed little but a worn-out pickup, a few skinny cattle, a mortgage, and several sections of desert which up until now nobody wanted. Pride and patriotism wouldn't let them shoot it out with the government, so the Department of Defense expropriated ranches and homes as bewildered, weather-beaten old cowhands stood by, "too tough to cry and too choked up to talk."

One of the last holdouts was James Cox, scion of tough and ornery W. W. Cox, whose ranch headquarters today sits on a knoll overlooking command headquarters at White Sands. Historically the site is San Agustín Springs. Nearby ruins indicate a possible Spanish influence. A hotel furnished accommodations for stagecoach travelers during the late 1850s. Here the Union forces in New Mexico under Major Lynde surrendered to Confederate Colonel John R. Baylor. Here also on October 7, 1899, in the very same Cox ranch house, Sheriff Pat Garrett, the tall slayer of Billy the Kid, and his deputy José Espalin, killed Norman Newman, a wanted outlaw.

By the 1930s, the Cox Ranch totaled about ninety thousand acres (130-150 sections) and was divided between James and Hal Cox, the sons of W. W. Cox. Hal took the third north of U.S. Route 70. The

Army Corps of Engineers filed condemnation procedures against both ranchers in 1945, quickly absorbing Hal's property as it was within a "dangerous impact area." Jim's position was tougher, although the "front yard" of his ranch house swiftly became the headquarters complex for White Sands Missile Range. The house and about nine thousand acres (12-14 sections) were spared, and remained in the Cox family possession because of its unique location. The headquarters complex fitted squarely between the main firing range and the Cox ranch house, which meant that to take it, the Army Corps of Engineers had to prove that the isolated building was in danger of being hit by a missile when the headquarters was not. Surprisingly, White Sands officials agreed, and supported Cox in this struggle. Not so surprising is that Jim Cox's relationship with military authorities today at White Sands is excellent. But he still smarts when someone mentions the Corps of Engineers.

But there were those who feared an insatiable governmental appetite for land. By mid 1951, sixty-seven V-2s had roared off the launching pad, flying higher and faster while gathering more and more information. Their accomplishments caused a few heads to wonder if the government's demand for additional land would ever end. Some residents complained that, based on Washington's past record, it would eventually own all of New Mexico. Subsequently, the civilians and the Army reached an agreement for co-use of any land acquired during future times, the ranchers staying on their property except during firing periods.

Today White Sands Missile Range is roughly one hundred miles long and forty miles wide, larger than Delaware, Rhode Island and the District of

Columbia combined. It begins just forty-five miles north of the Fort Bliss headquarters. There are four thousand square miles of government-owned land, and another four thousand square miles of co-use area. This does not include territory to accommodate longer-ranged vehicles, necessary since the mid 1950s. The Department of Defense selected a corridor heading northwest from White Sands toward Salt Lake City and Yakima, Washington. It terminates in Alaska.

However, such an extension has never been used. The longest firing distances have been from Utah to White Sands. In 1956 an Air Force Matador operating from Holloman Air Force Base, fired an air-to-ground rocket to Wendover Air Force Base in Utah. In 1963, an Air Force Hound Dog missile was launched from an aircraft flying in the vicinity of Del Rio, Texas. It impacted on White Sands Missile Range.

The testing and experimenting at White Sands have been of incalculable value to the free world's security. Thanks to all this, the American defensive arsenal is the strongest in the world. Nevertheless, while the successes at White Sands would fill volumes; the failures are the ones folks remember.

On May 29, 1947, a German scientist wired a gyroscope backwards on a four-and-one-half-ton experimental V-2. It lifted off and, instead of heading north, went south. Five minutes later it impacted a mile and a half south of Juárez. In 1963, a Pershing I missile took off from, and was supposed to have landed on, White Sands. Instead it hit near Creede, Colorado. A mounted missile posse of between thirty and forty horsemen spent over six months searching for it. Another Pershing I missile went astray from Blanding, Utah to White Sands. It struck the

White Sands Missile Range Headquarters near the foot of the rugged Organ Mountains of New Mexico. Missiles displayed are types which have been tested at White Sands. (White Sands Missile Range)

Navajo Reservation south of Farmington, New Mexico, and nobody could find it until the government offered a $500 reward. In September of 1967, a Pershing I missile flying from Utah smashed into Old Mexico just south of Van Horn, Texas.

The most controversial missile failure occurred in July, 1970. An Air Force Athena, a four-stage research missile used to study reentry phenomenon, left Green River, Utah, on its way to White Sands. However, it made an unscheduled side trip to near Torreon, Mexico, after the fourth stage prematurely ignited. The rocket hit in an uninhabited desert and buried itself in the sand. This missile, however, contained two small vials of Cobalt 57 for experimental purposes, a fact making the Mexicans very indignant and frustrated. They wanted to conduct a crash investigation, and did not have the facilities. Mexico reluctantly granted the State Department permission to criss-cross the site with detection equipment. After several yards of earth were found to be radioactive, the Americans dug up fifty-five barrels of dirt and stored them at White Sands where they are today. Altogether that stray missile cost the Air Force about $250,000 to recover.

After thirty-five years of firings, and 32,000 missile launchings, the fractional number of failures point out not the weaknesses in the system, but the strengths. Even more remarkable, there has never been an injury due to errant missiles impacting somewhere other than White Sands. Nowadays, scientists destroy these in flight, so unanticipated wanderings are considered unlikely. The erratic trails of smoke, common during missile failures of one, two and three decades ago, are rarely seen anymore by El Pasoans standing in their yards and looking north.

Today the V-2 is a relic, a museum piece. Yet it represented the first large-scale rocket program at White Sands, and it is the grandfather of America's family of large missiles. The five year V-2 experimental program conducted by Wernher von Braun gave birth to America's large missiles including the Corporal, Redstone, Nike, Aerobee, Atlas and Pershing. The experiments also directly led to the Neptune, Aries, Viking, Athena, Copperhead, Lance, Hawk, Roland, and Tomahawk.

Scientific departments on White Sands Missile Range have such jawbreaking titles as United States Army Atmospheric Sciences Laboratory (ASL), Office of Missile Electronic Warfare (OMEW), United States TRADOC Systems Analysis Activity (TRASANA), United States Naval Ordnance Missile Test Facility (NOMTF), and National Aeronautics and Space Administration (NASA). These units build and install vast communications networks. They study how one missile might shoot down another. They analyze deep probes into space. Work has been done on the Apollo radar, Gemini laser, and parachute air drops. Experiments have been undertaken with the new Cruise missile. And White Sands Missile Base is an alternate landing site for the Space Shuttle. Instrumentation support has been given NASA's Project Mercury flights and Gemini space shots.

One of the most exciting and controversial programs is the High Energy Laser (HEL) project. Designed for completion in 1983 at a cost of $25 million, it seeks to determine just how lethal a laser system can be against a target. While the system has its prominent critics, should tests prove the laser feasible as a surgical weapon, the project will add vast new dimensions to military defense.

A V-2 rocket supports a "WAC Corporal" on top as it thunders into the blue at White Sands Missile Range. These first multi-stage rockets were called "Bumpers." (White Sands Missile Range)

White Sands is one of twenty-six major test facilities operated by the Department of Defense. While the Army is the chief beneficiary of these tests, the base also serves the Navy, Air Force, and NASA. The White Sands Missile Range is under operational control of the United States Test and Evaluation Command (TECOM), with headquarters at Aberdeen Proving Ground, Maryland.

The site has become the most highly instrumented range in the free world. Sophisticated computer systems process and correlate the voluminous data, providing scientists and range users with timely and reliable performance records.

The base is a city unto itself with housing, offices, barber shops, restaurants, shopping places, recreation areas. One rarely hears German spoken anymore except among visitors. One does hear a lot of Spanish since it is the first language of many employees.

The nearly eight thousand men and women who operate White Sands (over ninety percent being civilians) are a new generation. They stand on portions of the most historic land on earth, the hills and valleys where prehistoric Indians once hunted the buffalo, where gunfighters stalked each other at High Noon, and they look into the heavens and dream of vast new frontiers.

16

Defender of the Free World

OTHER THAN BEING a source of employment and government money, few Army posts have done more for a city than has Fort Bliss for El Paso. It has been the protector in times of battle, the savior in times of natural disaster, the benefactor in times of changing world conditions. It has purchased land (occasionally from unwilling sellers), trained El Paso soldiers and provided sports.

Fort Bliss assisted El Pasoans during the great flood of 1897, not only salvaging possessions but furnishing shelter and food. The same chivalry existed during the flood of 1925. This time the soldiers also guarded a huge pile of family belongings in Washington Park.

Fort Bliss has come a long way since it was the Post Opposite El Paso in 1849. In those days its mission was easily defined: to stand guard against the Indian and to attack him wherever he might be found. In a sense its mission is much the same, the difference being that Fort Bliss stands guard over the entire free world. The Indian is now a friend, but different enemies, if not necessarily beyond the next hill, are certainly over the next ocean.

The new Fort Bliss arose from the ashes of World War I. Air defense became an important part of war, and antiaircraft training a vital part of Fort Bliss. However, the ability of guns to shoot with increasing accuracy and more distance always lagged behind the capability of aircraft to fly higher and faster.

By September, 1940, when the Antiaircraft Training Center was established, the National Guard moved in. The 202nd Regiment from Illinois, the 206th Regiment from Arkansas, and the 260th Regiment from the District of Columbia were a few to set up camp. One of the toughest was the 200th Coast Artillery from New Mexico. In late 1941 and early 1942, it would hold out for three bloody months on Bataan and Corregidor, firing everything it had at wave after wave of Japanese planes. Finally, there was no ammunition left to shoot, and over two thousand men of the proud 200th surrendered. Their subsequent suffering in the Bataan Death March is a legendary if tragic story in military history.

In 1941, the 1st Tow Target Squadron arrived, its task being to tow gliders and radio controlled drones to where the antiaircraft gunners could practice. To make things easier, the Antiaircraft School moved from North Carolina to Fort Bliss in 1944, and the antiaircraft artillery people controlled the post following the departure of the 1st Cavalry Division.

An expanding post such as Fort Bliss had its own burial ground, officially the Fort Bliss National Cemetery as of Armistice Day, November 11, 1936. Since those early times the cemetery has expanded to fifty-nine acres, forty-three of which are currently in use. The old "Post Section" in the southeast corner has four acres. As of the early 1980s, there are approximately sixteen thousand former active duty personnel, veterans and dependents buried at Fort Bliss. Old Indian scouts lie there along with eighteen Chinese pilots killed while training in the United States during World War II. Also included are a number of German and Italian prisoners of war who died while interned in Southwestern camps from 1943 through 1945.

The story of these POW's is obscure. About 425,000 Italians were imprisoned in the United States, several thousand in the El Paso Southwest. Texas had over sixty camps, New Mexico about twenty-five.

Approximately a thousand Italian prisoners came to El Paso in August, 1943, from a camp in Lordsburg, New Mexico, and were housed for nearly six months in the El Paso County Coliseum before being transferred to Fort Bliss. While living in the coliseum, the volunteers picked cotton on lower valley farms, drawing the prevailing wage of $1.50 per hundred pounds of short staple cotton and $3 for every hundred pounds of long staple cotton. However, they were paid in stockade canteen credits, not in money. Unused funds were credited to individual accounts. When Italy surrendered and then declared war on Germany in late 1943, most Italians at Fort Bliss joined the American army and were permitted to serve in all military categories except combat.

Germans joined the Italians at Fort Bliss POW camps in 1944, a thousand being interned at Bliss,

Retreat is perhaps the most honored ceremony at Fort Bliss. Each evening at five o'clock, the United States flag is carefully lowered and put away until the following morning. This particular ceremony is taking place at Pershing Circle on Fort Bliss. (Sterling Brooks)

plus Ysleta and Fabens, Texas, and Las Cruces, Hatch and Lordsburg, New Mexico. The Germans picked cotton on valley farms too, while performing skilled and unskilled labor on post.

Meanwhile, thousands of El Pasoans went off to war, and 558 did not come back. PFC Silvestre Herrera won the Medal of Honor with the 142nd Infantry in Mertzwiller, France. Lieutenant William D. Hawkins did the same with a Marine Assault Regiment at Tarawa in the South Pacific. Navy Pharmacist Mate Charles V. Porras, a graduate of Ysleta High School, posthumously won the Navy Cross and Purple Heart when the 1st Marine Division stormed Peleliu Island.

In 1972 the El Paso City Council voted to erect a memorial flagpole at Scenic Point in El Paso. A United States flag now waves day and night in honor of those who gave their lives in World War II, Korea and Vietnam. At the unveiling ceremony, Mayor Bert Williams dedicated the flagpole to Lieutenant Chris P. Fox, Jr., a graduate of El Paso High School, who won the Bronze Star, three Battle Stars and the Purple Heart for action with the 273rd Infantry, and who died in Europe during the Battle of the Bulge.

Numerous other heroes survived. Lieutenant Gabriel Navarrete (now Major in the United States Army Reserve), a graduate of Cathedral High School, won the Distinguished Service Cross, two Silver Stars and seven Purple Hearts for action with the 141st Infantry in the Mediterranean.

Then came July 16, 1945, and the world's first atomic bomb blast northwest of Alamogordo, New Mexico. The war was within a short time of being over, and Fort Bliss would make a transition back to peace.

On August 3, 1944, Headquarters Army Ground Forces ordered the Antiaircraft Artillery School from Camp Davis, North Carolina to Fort Bliss. Two years later the school started several significant programs. It directed the 1st Antiaircraft Artillery and Guided Missile Battalion to perform operational testing on various existing and prototype rockets. The battalion participated in the first American firing of a German V-2 rocket at White Sands in September, 1946. The Department of Guided Missiles was formed.

Two months later the Antiaircraft Artillery School was redesignated the Antiaircraft and Guided Missile Branch. Early in 1947, it fired its first all-American missile, the WAC Corporal.

While modern rocketry began with the experiments of Dr. Robert H. Goddard during the 1930s, and expanded with the Germans and their V-2s, the system would never have grown beyond rudimentary phases without an evolution starting in 1944 of a radical new weapons system. It amounted to two technological breakthroughs: radar which made it possible to instantly measure the distance to any aircraft, and the development of electronic computers. Weapons progressed to the 40mm, 90mm and 120mm cannons, and then into the DIVAD gun system and a 20mm electronic gatling gun, the Vulcan.

On July 1, 1957, the United States Army Antiaircraft Artillery and Guided Missile Center was redesignated as the United States Army Air Defense Center at Fort Bliss. The artillery school officially became the United States Army Air Defense School as Fort Bliss entered the age of Nike Ajax, Nike Hercules, Hawk, Sprint, Chaparral and Redeye. The LaCrosse and Honest John were surface-to-surface

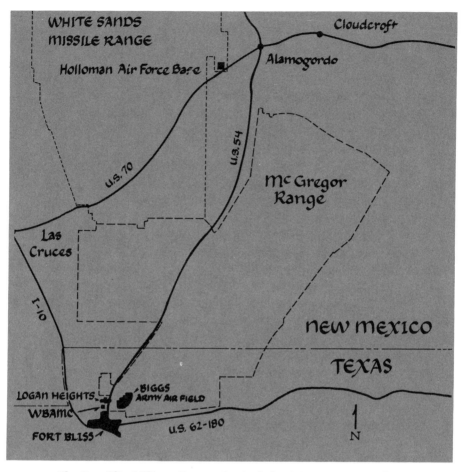

The Fort Bliss Military Reservation includes 1,130,000 acres. The property, part owned and part leased, is roughly seventy-five miles long and fifty-four miles wide. (Placido Cano)

missile systems not taught at Fort Bliss but at Fort Sill, Oklahoma. These units frequently visit Bliss for firing practice.

With the advent of the Nike, the free world had a guidance system capable of hitting an evasive, high-flying target, to literally outmaneuver an airplane.

For the first time in history, a weapon was not dependent upon being pointed in a specific direction. Then in July, 1960, came another memorable first. An army Hawk destroyed a Little John missile.

Air Defense had so many students in 1950 that a $10 million appropriation led to construction of thirty-one three-story, permanent-type barracks and six motor parks. In November, 1954, Hinman Hall was dedicated as school headquarters, built at a cost of $2.5 million. In the spring of 1958, approximately $4,448,000 worth of new building was announced, including $250,000 for a materials laboratory. Two additional wings of a classroom building cost $5 million. A $1,857,000 radar park went in with sixteen guided missile laboratory and classroom buildings.

However, a controversy started with a $3 million expansion of range facilities beginning in 1953. Red Canyon Range in the San Andres Mountains of southern New Mexico came into existence. Nearly three thousand Nike Ajax missiles were fired there before Red Canyon was replaced by McGregor Range, which had as its core the 193,000 acres (300 sections) belonging to Malcolm and J. Douglas McGregor. The area was east of Orogrande, New Mexico. The Army leased the land beginning in 1954, but with the announcement of public hearings in Alamogordo, New Mexico by the House Armed Services Committee, the Army demanded it all.

The military took land belonging to Oliver Lee, Tom Bell, Charlie Bassett, and a host of other ranchers. Most cowmen sold out quietly, but eighty-two year old John Prather was not "most" cowmen. He loved this land abutting the south slopes of the Sacramento Mountains. His family had lived there since 1883. When condemnation proceedings started at Albuquerque in July, 1956, John adjusted his thick lenses, cradled his rifle and said, "You can bury me, but you can't move me."

When his ninety-day grace was up, Prather was still at home. It was extremely frustrating for the government. One crusty, stubborn old man was catching the imagination of the country, and the Army could not afford to make a martyr of him.

The military cranked up a publicity campaign to demonstrate how necessary that land was for national defense. A Rocket Symposium was announced for April 26, 1957. McGregor Range would be dedicated and missiles fired, all for the viewing public's benefit. However, several politicians including Congressman Clair Engle of California expressed alarm that the Army wanted too much of New Mexico, that more and more land was leaving the tax rolls and each new acquisition left the state smaller and poorer. Even New Mexico Senator Clinton Anderson, recognizing a vote-getting issue when he saw one, criticized the Army for moving onto a range without a clear title. Obviously embarrassed, Secretary of Army Wilbur Brucker cancelled the exercise.

John Prather had now done what Indians, Mexican bandits, and two European wars could never do. Without firing a shot, he forced the Army to back down. In August, Judge Waldo Rogers exempted Prather's house and fifteen acres from military seizure. It was a victory for both sides, of sorts.

Gradually the McGregor Guided Missile Range became the largest inland air defense region in the free world. By the early 1980s, it encompassed 1,089 square miles (697,472 acres) in New Mexico, all of it adjacent to and twenty-six miles northeast of Fort Bliss headquarters. Air defense batteries from the United States, Japan, Spain, Kuwait and Jordan

Fort Bliss includes five thousand buildings and a billion dollars worth of land, structures and equipment. (Frank Mangan)

Hinman Hall is headquarters for the U. S. Army Air Defense Center and the Air Defense School. It houses offices of the commanding general and staff, plus several classrooms and laboratories of the Air Defense School. (Sterling Brooks)

The Main Exchange on Fort Bliss. (Frank Mangan)

Tree-shaded homes house high-ranking Fort Bliss officers and families along Sheridan Road. (Frank Mangan)

started annual firings at McGregor. The 3rd Armored Cavalry's Cobra attack helicopters practiced aerial gunnery there.

Other ranges are currently supporting McGregor. The Dona Ana Range Camp, for example, is on the west slope of the Organ Mountains, New Mexico, about twenty-seven miles northwest of the Fort Bliss main post. It contains approximately 450 square miles. Each year Fort Bliss trains between 8,000 and 16,000 national guardsmen and reservists there. The 3rd Armored Cavalry uses the Dona Ana facilities for tank gunnery practice.

North McGregor, oftentimes known as the Orogrande Range, is fifty-eight miles northeast of Fort Bliss headquarters and seven miles east of the New Mexico village of Orogrande. It supports the Redeye/Chaparral missile firings, many of which impact on White Sands Missile Range.

From an economic and geographic point of view, Castner Range has been long known to El Pasoans. Located along the eastern side of the Franklin Mountains, the range was acquired by Fort Bliss during the 1920s and 1930s. By the 1960s, the city of El Paso had expanded to the edges of Castner, and even leapfrogged it in some places. As a result, Fort Bliss donated and sold much of Castner back to the community during the 1970s and 1980s, the property going for municipal, county, state and federal projects, and for construction of the North-South Freeway.

Logan Heights lies on the edge of this activity, three miles north of the main post. It has supported combat basic training at Fort Bliss since November, 1951. The training was discontinued in 1955, restarted in 1956, and discontinued once more in 1957. The Department of the Army reactivated it on Sep-

This commemorative stamp was issued in 1948 to honor the Fort Bliss centennial. In those days, letters were mailed for three cents. (Frank Mangan Collection)

tember 17, 1965, closed it in 1969, and resurrected it once more in 1975. Since 1980 it has been called One Station Unit Training, which means that a recruit is guaranteed an opportunity to stay with his unit once he leaves basic.

Fort Bliss in the 1980s is primarily a training installation whose five major missions are: to develop combat doctrine and training material for air defense forces, conduct basic and advanced training, see that squads, platoons, batteries and battalions can perform their duties, maintain military units at a high state of readiness, and support annual service firings on the McGregor Range complex.

To help implement this, Fort Bliss looks forward to a new assortment of weapons. The Patriot, a high and medium altitude missile, can attack and destroy aircraft while tracking scores more. The Roland, ground based like the Patriot, will track and destroy up to ten enemy aircraft. The Division Air Defense Gun System (DIVAD) has the capability to defend the Army's forward units against air attacks. The Stinger, which replaces the Redeye, is a shoulder-fired infrared homing missile capable of providing defensive coverage against airplanes harassing small combat units in the field. A follow-up weapon of advanced design is the Post, currently undergoing engineering tests. Many of these systems will become operational by the mid 1980s.

A very significant part of the Air Defense School at Fort Bliss is its liaison component, which includes Air Force and Marine representatives. There are allied officers from Canada, France, Germany, Japan, Jordan, Denmark, the Netherlands, the United Kingdom, Kuwait and the Republic of Korea, the largest of which is the German contingent. Since

174

Entrance to Fort Bliss replica. The museum, a cluster of adobe buildings, and a gift from the people of El Paso, was opened in 1948, the 100th anniversary of the post. The cross is in error, as the original of this particular building never served as a chapel. (Sterling Brooks)

The U. S. Air Defense Artillery arsenal depends on sophisticated missile systems such as the Patriot. (Fort Bliss Public Affairs Office)

Drill sergeants play integral part in basic training. (Sterling Brooks)

1953, the Fort Bliss Air Defense School has graduated over 220,000 students, ten percent from foreign countries.

Other organizations are the 11th Air Defense Artillery Brigade and the 3rd Armored Cavalry Regiment. The former is charged with maintaining combat readiness in personnel, logistics and training. The 3rd Armored Cavalry continuously trains as a reinforcer for American combat troops in Germany. It frequently visits Germany for maneuvers.

Fort Bliss functions under the Training and Doctrine Command (TRADOC) with headquarters in Fort Monroe, Virginia. However, the strategic army forces, such as the 3rd Armored Cavalry and the 11th Air Defense Artillery Brigade, are subordinate to Forces Command (FORSCOM), whose headquarters are in Fort McPherson, Georgia.

Fort Bliss currently includes 1,130,000 acres, nearly five thousand buildings and approximately a billion dollars worth of land, structures and equipment. The property, part owned and part leased, is roughly seventy-five miles long and fifty-four miles wide. The buildings include Van Horne Park with 801 family housing units, and the Capehart housing project with 410 units, both constructed in 1958. Biggs Army Air Field, the Air Defense Museum, the Non-Commissioned Officers Museum, the 3rd Armored Cavalry Regimental Museum, and the Fort Bliss Replica Museum, dedicated in 1948, are also a part of Bliss.

Fort Bliss became home to General of the Army Omar N. Bradley in 1977. Five star generals do not retire, so General Bradley remained on active duty until his death in 1981. His offices and residence were on Medical Center property, and he regularly visited with miltiary and civilian personnel.

Insignia of the U. S. Army Air Defense Center.

Insignia of the 11th Air Defense Artillery Brigade.

Insignia of the U. S. Army Air Defense School.

Fort Bliss is now mature enough for a calm assessment of its past, but young enough to look forward to the future.

Some of the adjustments are taken so much for granted that it is difficult to recall a time when things were not like they are now. The integration of blacks and whites has been especially significant, these revolutionary changes having occurred since the late 1940s and early 1950s. Both races now live, work, play and study together, blacks being found in all job classifications and ranks, equal and not separate. The system has contributed not only to the welfare of the people involved but to the security of the country.

Since World War II, and especially since the Korean War, the number of women soldiers at Fort Bliss and indeed the entire American armed forces have increased dramatically. While they are still a minority, women fill every job description including drill instructors. They operate the missile systems, march on maneuvers, educate the students. It is just a matter of time until Fort Bliss has a female commanding general.

As of early 1980, there were approximately 20,000 military and 7,000 civilians at Fort Bliss. Their dependents numbered 25,000. Nearly 15,000 military retirees now live in El Paso, and these have an estimated 27,000 dependents. The Fort Bliss civilian and military payroll is in excess of $303.2 million and when all the moneys spent are totaled, the economic impact on El Paso exceeds $500 million each year.

Today, Fort Bliss is as different from its 1849 beginnings as Planet Earth is from the frozen moons of Jupiter. It has grown from a rudimentary frontier

The Hawk is a medium-range, all weather guided missile system designed to provide air defense coverage against low-to-medium-altitude air attack. The Hawk is a towed missile.
(Fort Bliss Public Affairs Office)

The Chaparral is a surface-to-air, infrared homing missile capable of intercepting a hostile aircraft at low altitudes in fair weather and under visual observation conditions. (Fort Bliss Public Affairs Office)

The Stinger is a man-portable, shoulder-fired, infrared homing (heat-seeking) air defense guided missile system. It is designed to counter high-speed, low-level, ground-attack aircraft.
(Fort Bliss Public Affairs Office)

Army post with its size presently counted in numbers of square miles rather than acres; its personnel counted in the thousands rather than hundreds.

Sprinkler systems have replaced the water wagons, modern cars roll softly by where wagons used to squeak. The base has several times as many dependents as it used to have soldiers. There are shops, schools, movie theaters, bowling alleys, offices, warehouses, churches and museums. The streets are paved, the houses quiet, the yards watered and manicured. The post is as much a part of town as any neighborhood, ten minutes by freeway from downtown.

Bullets have been largely replaced by missiles. The trusty weapons of a century ago, or even twenty-five years ago, are now museum pieces. Maturing in a number of wars, Fort Bliss is a powerful, confident, alert giant, a cornerstone of the free world.

German Air Force

TEN YEARS AFTER World War II, Germany had established a credible armed force and had begun to think in terms of air defense. By January, 1956, German army officers began arriving at Fort Bliss for air defense training, as a rule taking the Artillery Officers Basic Course.

Meanwhile, they created their own training commands in Germany. The first *Bundeswehr* (Air Defense) unit was activated on January 1, 1956. By July, 1957, an Air Defense Artillery school opened at Rendsburg, the soldiers drilling predominately with 40mm L70 Air Defense weapons. Still, the Germans needed more expertise and experience, advantages belonging to the Americans. So on November 9, 1957, the Germans established an Air Defense Liaison Office at Fort Bliss. It arranged the training of German soldiers.

From 1958 through 1961, key German personnel trained on the Nike system at Fort Bliss, and until 1965 on the Hawk system. The Germans also established the German Air Force Air Defense School (GAFADS) for the Nike missile at Aachen in October, 1964. However, the introduction of Hawk missiles carried with it the creation of another school, a project not cost effective. So GAFADS transferred its command to Fort Bliss where the Germans currently train on the Nike and Hawk. While the United States is phasing out the Nike Hercules, several of America's NATO allies including Germany, are not.

The GAFADS permanent party at Fort Bliss consists of approximately three hundred Germans of all ranks and job descriptions. They train approximately twelve hundred of their countrymen annually.

Another six hundred Germans are taught by the United States Army Air Defense School, the United States Army Missile and Munitions Center School, and the United States Army Field Artillery School. Although a few training units are at Redstone Arsenal, Alabama, and at Fort Sill, Oklahoma, Fort Bliss is still considered home base. The Federal Republic of Germany pays all costs.

The 3rd
Armored Cavalry

FEW UNITS in the United States Army have a record as long and as unblemished as the 3rd Armored Cavalry. It was organized in 1846 as The Regiment of Mounted Riflemen. During the Mexican War, the regiment fought in six campaigns, the last one taking it over the walls of Chapultepec.

After the war, the regiment served in various locations. It went to Jefferson Barracks, Missouri, in 1848, and transferred to Oregon Territory in 1849. By May, 1851, it was back in Jefferson Barracks, only to be moved in December to Texas. In 1853, it was redesignated as the 1st Regiment of Mounted Riflemen.

Indian troubles called the 3rd to New Mexico in 1856. For the next four years it operated from West Texas, to Colorado, Arizona, New Mexico, Nevada and Utah. Then in 1861, with many officers and enlisted men joining the South, the 1st Regiment of Mounted Riflemen was redesignated as the 3rd Cavalry Regiment. Throughout the War Between the States, the regiment fought in New Mexico, Tennessee, Mississippi, Alabama and North Carolina. It participated in the Chattanooga campaign as part of the advance guard for General Sherman's army.

From 1866 through 1870, it fought Indians in New Mexico, and in 1871 was transferred to the Department of the Platte, which included Wyoming, Montana, the Dakotas and Nebraska. During 1876 the regiment served in the Big Horn and Yellowstone campaigns against the Sioux and Cheyenne. It fought in the Battle of Rosebud Creek. After that, it returned to Arizona and participated in the last Apache wars.

The unit saw action in Cuba, charged San Juan Hill, and helped suppress the Philippine insurrection. Although it served in Europe, the regiment took very little part in World War I. However, during World War II, it fought with distinction, and was one of the first units to enter Germany.

After undergoing several name changes during the Second World War, the unit became the 3rd Armored Cavalry Regiment on November 5, 1948. During the next two decades, the 3rd Armored Cavalry moved throughout the United States and Europe, coming to Fort Bliss in 1972 from Fort Lewis, Washington. Although the regiment's training takes place in a desert environment, it is expected to move, shoot and communicate in the climate and terrain of northern and central Europe.

Appendix

Fort Bliss Commanders

Major Jefferson Van Horne	1849-1851
Lieut. Colonel E. B. Alexander	1854
Lieut. Colonel John B. Magruder	1855
Major James Longstreet	1855
Major John T. Sprague	1855
Major T. H. Holmes	1856
Lieut. Colonel Issac V. D. Reeve	1857-1859
Major T. H. Holmes	1859
Captain W. L. Elliot	1859
Captain E. G. Walker	1859
First Lieutenant Thomas K. Jackson	1859-1860
Captain Thomas G. Pitcher	1860
First Lieutenant Thomas K. Jackson	1860-1861
Lieut. Colonel Isaac V. D. Reeve	1861
Lieut. Colonel John R. Baylor	1861
Brigadier General H. H. Sibley	1861-1862
Brigadier General James H. Carleton	1862-1863
Major William McMullen	1863
Colonel George W. Bowie	1864
Major Joseph Smith	1865
Captain David H. Brotherton	1865-1866
Major William R. Gerhart	1866
Captain E. C. Mason	1866-1868
Major H. C. Merriam	1869
Captain F. M. Crandall	1870
Captain C. Bentzoni	1871
Captain F. M. Cox	1872-1874
Major Z. R. Bliss	1875-1876
Major N. W. Osborne	1878-1880
Captain H. R. Brinkerhoff	1881
Captain O. W. Bollock	1882
Major J. S. Fletcher	1883
Major H. S. Hawkins	1884-1885
Captain Gregory Barrett	1886

Colonel M. M. Blunt	1887
Captain E. P. Ewers	1888
Colonel N. W. Osborne	1889-1890
Major J. Henton	1891-1892
Colonel H. M. Lazelle	1893
Captain W. H. McLaughlin	1893-1894
Colonel D. Parker	1895
Colonel D. D. Van Valzah	1896-1898
Lieutenant N. F. McClure	1898
Major Churchill Towles	1898
Captain Joseph F. Nichols	1898-1899
Captain S. L. Woodward	1899
Captain H. R. H. Loughborough	1899-1901
Captain F. M. Caldwell	1901
Lieut. Colonel H. H. Adams	1901-1902
Lieut. Colonel C. P. Terrett	1902
Lieut. Colonel H. L. Haskell	1902
Lieut. Colonel H. S. Foster	1903-1904
Captain H. M. Dickman	1904
Major Ammon A. Augur	1904-1906
Major J. M. T. Partello	1906
Colonel R. W. Hoyt	1906-1907
Captain S. Burkhardt, Jr.	1907
Colonel J. F. Huston	1907-1910
Colonel A. C. Sharpe	1910
Colonel E. F. Glenn	1910-1912
Colonel E. Z. Steever	1912
Colonel Frank West	1912-1913
Colonel Joseph Gerrard	1914
Brigadier General Hugh Scott	1914
Brigadier General John J. Pershing	1914-1916
Brigadier General George Bell	1916
Colonel John W. Heard	1917
Colonel William D. Beach	1917
Colonel George T. Langhorne	1917
Colonel Edward Anderson	1917-1918
Brigadier General Robert L. Howze	1918
Brigadier General James J. Hornbrook	1918
Major General Robert L. Howze	1918-1925
Brigadier General Joseph C. Castner	1925-1926
Brigadier General Edwin D. Winans	1926-1927
Brigadier General George V. H. Moseley	1928-1929

Brigadier General George Barnhart	1930
Brigadier General Walter C. Short	1930-1932
Major General Frank McCoy	1933
Brigadier General Walter C. Short	1934-1935
Brigadier General Hamilton Hawkins	1936
Brigadier General Ben Lear	1937
Brigadier General Kenyon Joyce	1938
Brigadier General Robert C. Richardson, Jr.	1939-1941
Major General Innis P. Swift	1941
Colonel Frederick D. Griffith	1941-1942
Colonel Edgar B. Taulbee	1942
Colonel M. H. Tomlinson	1943
Colonel John K. Brown	1944-1945
Colonel Frank L. Whittaker	1945
Colonel George J. Forster	1945
Colonel Robert H. Van Volkenburgh	1946
Major General John L. Homer	1946-1950
Major General John T. Lewis	1950-1952
Brigadier General F. L. Hayden	1952
Lieut. General Stanley R. Mickelsen	1952-1954
Major General Paul W. Rutledge	1954-1956
Major General Robert J. Wood	1956-1957
Major General Sam C. Russell	1957-1961
Major General Marshall S. Carter	1961-1962
Brigadier General Stephen M. Mellnik	1962
Major General Tom V. Stayton	1962-1965
Major General George T. Powers III	1965-1967
Major General George V. Underwood, Jr.	1967-1968
Major General Richard T. Cassidy	1968-1971
Major General Raymond L. Shoemaker	1971-1973
Major General C. J. LeVan	1973-1976
Major General Robert J. Lunn	1976-1977
Major General John J. Koehler, Jr.	1977-1979
Major General John B. Oblinger, Jr.	1979-1982
Major General James P. Maloney	1982-1985
Major General Donald R. Infante	1985-

William Beaumont Army Hospital Commanders

Colonel William R. Eastman	1921-1922
Colonel M. A. W. Shockley	1922-1927
Colonel Reuben Miller	1927-1928
Colonel William H. Moncrief	1928-1931
Colonel Henry F. Pipes	1931-1937
Colonel George M. Edwards	1937-1945
Colonel George W. Reyer	1945-1948
Colonel James E. Yarborough	1948-1951
Colonel Walter C. Rayals	1951-1952
Colonel Abner Zelm	1953-1957
Brigadier General L. Holmes Ginn	1957-1958
Brigadier General Clinton S. Lyter	1958-1960
Brigadier General James B. Stapleton	1960-1965
Major General Robert E. Blount	1965-1966
Brigadier General Frederic J. Hughes, Jr.	1966-1967
Brigadier General James A. Wier	1967-1968
Major General Kenneth D. Orr	1968-1970
Brigadier General Robert M. Hardaway	1970-1975
Major General Charles G. Pixley	1975-1976
Major General Raymond H. Bishop	1976-1979
Brigadier General Kenneth A. Cass	1979-1980
Brigadier General Chester L. Ward	1980-1982
Brigadier General John Major	1983-1986
Brigadier General Richard D. Cameron	1986-

White Sands Missile Range Commanders

Colonel Harold R. Turner	1945-1947
Brigadier General Philip G. Blackmore	1947-1950
Brigadier General George G. Eddy	1950-1954

Major General William L. Bell	1954-1956
Major General Waldo E. Laidlaw	1956-1960
Major General John G. Shinkle	1960-1962
Major General J. Frederick Thorlin	1962-1965
Major General John M. Cone	1965-1966
Major General Horace G. Davisson	1966-1970
Major General Edward H. deSaussure	1970-1972
Major General Arthur H. Sweeney	1972-1974
Major General Robert J. Proudfoot	1974-1975
Major General Orville L. Tobiason	1975-1979
Major General Duard D. Ball	1979-1980
Major General Alan A. Nord	1980-1982
Major General Niles J. Fulwyler	1982-1986
Major General Joe S. Owens	1986-1987
Major General Thomas J. P. Jones	1987-

Colonel Karl F. Eklund served as acting commander between Major General Cone's death and Major General Davisson's assumption of command.

Acknowledgments

The editors of this book wish to thank the following persons and institutions for their assistance.

Fort Bliss personnel read and commented on portions of the manuscript and aided in supplying and identifying photographs. We are pleased for the suggestions and guidance of Lieut. Colonel Edward M. McDonald, Public Affairs Officer, and his topnotch associates, Jim Lemons and Ed Starnes. At the Fort Bliss Replica Museum, our thanks to curator Margarita Blanco, Joe Ramirez, Charles Duncan and Rob Edwards. Sergeants Scott Hamrick and Tom Butcher of the 3rd Armored Cavalry Museum provided valuable help. Colonel Sydney Baird, representative of the U.S. Air Force aided in identifying photographs. Our thanks also to Gina Calvano at the German Air Force Defense School and to personnel at the Air Defense Artillery Museum.

At White Sands Missile Range we were fortunate to get some very fine assistance. Chief among those who helped were Major David Olmstead, Public Affairs Officer, and his knowledgeable associate James Lovelady. Tom Starkweather, Chief, Operations Branch Data Science Division, took time out to read the White Sands chapter and offer his comments, as did Austin Vick, Chief of the Data Collection Division. Marion Shropshire, Chief of the Real Time Computer Branch guided us through the fascinating Range Control Center. For an excellent selection of photographs we thank Bill Gross and Debbie Bingham at the Public Affairs Office.

At William Beaumont Army Medical Center we are grateful for the services of Major John R. Rachfal, Chief of Plans, Operations and Training. Major Rachfal read and made suggestions regarding the Beaumont chapter. Other helpful Beaumont persons were Dorothy Wallen and Lieut. Colonel Margaret Baker, Chief of the Occupational Therapy Section.

Special thanks also go to Dr. C. L. Sonnichsen who read portions of the manuscript, and to Bill Schilling, Cheryl Metz, and Martha Peterson, superb grammarians and proofreaders.

Others who assisted were Jay Smith, frontier military historian, W. E. "Sandy" Sanford, editor of *Air Defense Magazine*, Major General (USA-Ret.) Frederic J. Hughes, who read the medical portion of the manuscript and Mrs. Harriot Howze Jones, daughter of former Fort Bliss commander, Major General Robert Lee Howze. S. H. "Bud" Newman of the University of Texas at El Paso library archives was very helpful, as was Tom Burdett, head of the S.L.A. Marshall Collection of Military History.

At the El Paso Public Library we are indebted to Itoko McNully and Danny Escontrias of the Southwest Section, and Mary Sarber of Library Management.

Those who shared important material and information include Bill Hooten, former editor of *The El Paso Times*; Frank Hemingway, now retired from White Sands Missile Range; Robb Cox, manager of the Cox Ranch at St. Agustín Springs, New Mexico; Virginia Turner and Trini Acosta of the *El Paso Herald-Post*; Baltazar Alvarez of *The El Paso Times*; Bill Newkirk of the El Paso Convention and Visitors Bureau; Cliff Trussell of The El Paso Company; David Shindo and John Ireland of Darst-Ireland Photography; photojournalist Sterling Brooks, Warren Van Vorst, United States-Mexico International Boundary and Water Commission, El Paso County Historical Society, and Pioneer Association of El Paso.

Also, Colonel (USA-Ret.) M. H. Thomlinson, Chris P. Fox, Carl Hertzog, Dr. Rex Strickland, Dr. Haldeen Braddy, Ponsford Brothers Construction Company, Jane B. Perrenot, Colonel (USA-Ret.) James W. Ward, Lieut. Colonel (USA-Ret.) Tom Carson, John Cobb, Val M. Sorensen, Stacy C. Hinkle, Dale Walker, Conrey Bryson, Major (USA-Ret.) and Mrs. William Coonly, Colonel (USAF-Ret.) and Mrs. F. R. Lafferty, Colonel (USA-Ret.) H. Crampton Jones, Camille K. Craig, Colonel (USA-Ret.) and Mrs. James R. Spurrier, Lieut. Colonel (USA-Ret.) and Mrs. L. Lane Lee, Major General (USA-Ret.) and Mrs. William H. Nutter, Lieut. General (USA-Ret.) and Mrs. Hobart R. Gay, William Tole, Thomas Hanley, Paul Lange, Major General (USA-Ret.) and Mrs. James R. Pierce, Major (USA-Ret.) R. K. McMaster, Major (USA-Ret.) William Murray, Captain (USA-Ret.) Rudolph D. Delahanty, Lorena P. Edlen, Captain (USA-Ret.) and Mrs. Thomas J. Watts, Captain (USA-Ret.) James C. Cage, Lieut. Colonel (USA-Ret.) Arthur V. Crego, Colonel (USA-Ret.) and Mrs. Donald V. Schafbuch, Colonel (USA-Ret.) and Mrs. George G. Elms, Colonel (USA-Ret.) and Mrs. George B. Hudson, John G. Oechsner, Sr., Mr. and Mrs. Rayma L. Andrews, Alyce Brooks, Mary Van Haselen, Octavia Glasgow, Major General (USA-Ret.) J. W. Cunningham, John P. Shapp, and Colonel (USA-Ret.) and Mrs. Richard C. Singer.

Also, Major General (USA-Ret.) Terry de la Mesa Allen, Lieut. Colonel (USA-Ret.) Herman L. Alley, Colonel (USA-Ret.) Norman R. Archer, Carl A. Beers, Captain (USN-Ret.) John G. Boniface, Colonel (USA-Ret.) W. Craig Boyce, Jr., Major (USA-Ret.) Wm. H. Brown, Brigadier General (USA-Ret.) and Mrs. Wallace H. Brucker, Major General (USA-Ret.) Eugene F. Cardwell, Major (USA-Ret.) Joseph Carich, Lieut. General (USA-Ret.) Richard T. Cassidy, Mariano Castro, Captain (USA-Ret.) Daniel Catania, Omarie S. Cole, Major General (USA-Ret.) James L. Collins, Jr., Lieut. General (USAF-Ret.) Howard A. Craig, Flora H. Curd, Colonel (USA-Ret.) and Mrs. Samuel L. Davidson, Colonel (USA-Ret.) Francis Daugherty, Blanche R. Dorsey, Colonel (USA-Ret.) and Mrs. A. D. Dugan, Margaret Epps, Major (USA-Ret.) George K. Fell, Colonel (USA-Ret.) Urban F. George, Major (USA-Ret.) Dorothy C. Gerster, Mrs. Wm. W. Gordon, Herman A. Gschwind, Lieut. Colonel (USA-Ret.) Michael Halliday, Charlotte F. Hansen, Willa Hargrove, Mr. and Mrs. Paul Harvey, Sr., Colonel (USA-Ret.) and Mrs. James L. Hayden, Brigadier General (USA-Ret.) and Mrs. Earl W. Heathcote, Jane Davis Heffernan, Major General (USA-Ret.) Robert L. Howze, Jr., General (USA-Ret.) Hamilton H. Howze, Neppie B. Hutchinson, Colonel (USA-Ret.) and Mrs. Hans Kloepfer, Colonel (USA-Ret.) O. Paul Lance, Sr., Richard P. Langford, Chella V. P. Maloney, Lieut. Colonel (USA-Ret.) Robert J. McBrinn, Mary Jo McCoy, Wm. C. McGay, Robert E. McKee Construction Co., Lieut. Colonel (USA-Ret.) S. A. Merritt, Lieut. Colonel (USA-Ret.) Albert Merritt, Lieut. Commander (USN-Ret.) Allan W. Mills, Master Sergeant (USA-Ret.) James B. Murray, Colonel (USA-Ret.) Wm. H. Nealing, Howard C. Phelps, Colonel (USA-Ret.) and Mrs. Homer S. Pitzer, Jr., Major General (USA-Ret.) and Mrs. George T. Powers III, Gertrude S. Robinson, Dr. Bruno Rolak, Brigadier General (USA-Ret.) Ross H. Routh, Mr. and Mrs. Jay N. Saenger, Dr. Willard W. Schuessler, Merril B. Sharp, Colonel (USA-Ret.) Turner R. Sharp, Sr., Marcelino Serna, Lieut. General (USA-Ret.) Raymond L. Shoemaker, Wilfred D. Smithers, Colonel (USA-Ret.) Walter H. Stevenson, Mike Sullivan, Colonel (USA-Ret.) Wm. H. Sweet, Colonel (USA-Ret.) Walter D. Thomas, Curtiss M. Tuller, Colonel (USA-Ret.) Samuel P. Walker, Jr., Lieut. Colonel (USA-Ret.) Bertram C. Wright, Jessie Wuest, Carl D. W. Hays, Colonel (USA-Ret.) A. A. Frierson, and Brigadier General and Mrs. Archie Cannon.

Books

Agnew, S. C., *Garrisons of the Regular U.S. Army: New Mexico, 1846-1899* (Press of the Territorian, 1971).

Almada, Francisco R., *Diccionario Historia Geografia y Biografia* (University of Chihuahua, 1968).

Bartlett, John Russell, *Personal Narrative of Explorations and Incidents* (Rio Grande Press, 1965), two volumes.

Bernardo, C. J. and Eugene H. Bacon, *American Military Policy: Its Development Since 1775* (Military Service Publishing Co., 1957).

Billings, John S., *Hygiene of the United States Army with Descriptions of Military Posts* (Sol Lewis, 1974).

Braddy, Haldeen, *Pershing's Mission in Mexico* (Texas Western Press, 1966).

Brenner, Anita, *The Wind That Swept Mexico* (Texas, 1973).

Bryson, Conrey, *The Land Where We Live* (Aniversario del Paso, 1973).

Chandler, Lt. Col. Melbourne C., *Of Garryowen in Glory: The History of the 7th U.S. Cavalry* (Turnpike Press, 1960).

Chávez, Profr. Armando B., *Historia de Ciudad Juárez, Chih.* (Chihuahua, 1970).

Clendenen, Clarence C., *Blood on the Border: The United States Army and the Mexican Irregulars* (Macmillan, 1969).

Coleman, J. D., *The First Air Cavalry Division — Vietnam, Vol. I* (1970).

Connelley, William E., *Doniphan's Expedition* (Bryant & Douglas Book & Stationery Co., 1907).

Cutts, James M., *The Conquest of California and New Mexico* (Horn & Wallace, 1965).

Downey, Fairfax, *Indian-Fighting Army* (Scribners, 1941).

Faulk, Odie B., *Crimson Desert: Indian Wars of the Southwest* (Oxford, 1974).

———, *The Leather Jacket Soldier: Spanish Military Equipment and Institutions of the Late 18th Century* (Socio-Technical Publications, 1971).

Foner, Jack D., *The United States Soldier Between Two Wars: Army Life and Reforms, 1865-1898* (Humanities Press, 1970).

Frazer, Robert W. (Editor), *Mansfield on the Condition of Western Forts, 1853-54* (Oklahoma, 1963).

———, *Forts of the West* (Oklahoma, 1966).

Fugate, Francis L., *Frontier College: Texas Western at El Paso* (Texas Western Press, 1964).

Glass, Maj. E. L. N., *The Tenth Cavalry* (Old Army Press, 1972).

Hall, Martin Hardwick, *Sibley's New Mexico Campaign* (Texas, 1960).

————, *The Confederate Army in New Mexico* (Presidial Press, 1978).

Hart, Herbert M., *Old Forts of the Southwest* (Superior, 1964).

————, *Tour Guide to Old Western Forts* (Pruett, 1980).

Herr, John K. and Edward S. Wallace, *The Story of the U.S. Cavalry* (Little, Brown and Company, 1953).

Heyman, Max L., Jr., *Prudent Soldier: E. R. S. Canby, 1817-1873* (Arthur H. Clark, 1959).

Hinkle, Stacy C., *Wings and Saddles: The Air and Cavalry Expedition of 1919* (Texas Western Press, 1967).

————, *Wings Over the Border: The Army Air Service Armed Patrol of the United States-Mexico Border 1919-1921* (Texas Western Press, 1970).

Hunt, Aurora, *Major General James Henry Carleton: Western Frontier Dragoon, 1814-1873* (Arthur H. Clark, 1958).

Jones, Harriot Howze (Editor), *El Paso: A Centennial Portrait* (El Paso County Historical Society, 1973).

Knight, Oliver, *Following the Indian Wars* (Oklahoma, 1960).

————, *Life and Manners in the Frontier Army* (Oklahoma, 1978).

Kreidberg, Lt. Col. Marvin A. & Merton G. Henry, *History of Military Mobilization in the United States Army* (Department of the Army, 1955).

Lane, Lydia Spencer, *I Married A Soldier* (Horn & Wallace, 1964).

Leckie, William H., *The Buffalo Soldiers: A Narrative of the Negro Cavalry in the West* (Oklahoma, 1970).

Mangan, Frank, *El Paso In Pictures* (Mangan Books, 1971).

————, *Bordertown Revisited* (Mangan Books, 1973).

Martinez, Oscar J., *Border Boom Town: Ciudad Juarez Since 1848* (Texas, 1975).

Matloff, Maurice (Editor), *American Military History* (Chief of Military History, 1973).

McCall, Colonel George Archibald, *New Mexico in 1850: A Military View* (Oklahoma, 1968).

McMaster, Major Richard K., *Musket, Saber & Missile: A History of Fort Bliss* (Complete Printing, 1974).

Merrill, James M., *Spurs to Glory: The Story of the United States Cavalry* (Rand McNally, 1967).

Mills, Anson, *My Story* (Press of Byron S. Adams, Washington, 1921).

Mills, W. W., *Forty Years in El Paso* (Carl Hertzog, 1962).

Moorhead, Max L., *The Presidio: Bastion of the Spanish Borderlands* (Oklahoma, 1975).

Muller, William G., *The Twenty-Fourth Infantry* (Old Army Press, 1972).

Nankivell, John H., *Twenty-Fifth Infantry* (Old Army Press, 1972).

Neighbours, Kenneth Franklin, *Robert Simpson Neighbors and the Texas Frontier, 1836-1859* (Texian Press, 1975).

Porter, Eugene O., *San Elizario* (Jenkins Press, 1973).

———, *Letters of Ernst Kohlberg, 1875-1887* (Texas Western Press, 1973).

Pride, W. F., *The History of Fort Riley* (Pride, 1926).

Prucha, Francis Paul (Editor), *Army Life on the Western Frontier* (Oklahoma, 1958).

———, *A Guide to the Military Posts of the United States, 1789-1895* (State Historical Society of Wisconsin, 1964).

Rickey, Don Jr., *Forty Miles A Day on Beans and Hay* (Oklahoma, 1972).

Robinson, Willard B., *American Forts: Architectural Form and Function* (University of Illinois, 1977).

Roeder, Ralph, *Juarez and His Mexico* (Viking, 1947), two volumes.

Russell, Don, *Custer's Last* (Amon Carter Museum, 1968).

Ruth, Kent, *Great Day in the West: Forts, Posts and Rendezvous Beyond the Mississippi* (Oklahoma, 1963).

Sonnichsen, C. L., *The El Paso Salt War* (Texas Western Press, 1961).

———, *Tularosa: Last of the Frontier West* (Devin-Adair, 1963).

———, *Pass of the North* (Texas Western Press, 1969 and 1980), two volumes.

Sparrow, John C., *History of Personnel Demobilization in the United States Army* (Department of the Army, 1952).

Steele, James W., *Frontier Army Sketches* (New Mexico, 1969).

Strickland, Rex W., *El Paso in 1854: El Sabio Sembrador* (Texas Western Press, 1969).

Stubbs, Mary Lee, *Armor-Cavalry, Part 1: Regular Army and Army Reserve* (Chief of Military History, 1969).

Tate, James P. (Editor), *The American Military on the Frontier* (Office of Air Force History, 1978).

Thian, Raphael P., *Notes Illustrating the Military Geography of the United States, 1813-1880* (Texas, 1979).

Thomlinson, M. H., *The Garrison of Fort Bliss, 1849-1916* (Hertzog & Resler, 1945).

Turner, Timothy G., *Bullets, Bottles & Gardenias* (South-West Press, 1935).

Upton, Emory, *The Military Policy of the United States* (War Department, 1912).

Utley, Robert M., *Frontiersmen in Blue: The United States Army and the Indian, 1848-1865* (Macmillan, 1967).

———, *Frontier Regulars: The United States Army and the Indian, 1866-1890* (Macmillan, 1973).

Vandiver, Frank E., *Black Jack: The Life and Times of John J. Pershing* (Texas A&M, 1977).

Weighley, Russell F., *History of the United States Army* (Macmillan, 1967).

Winsor, Bill, *Texas In the Confederacy: Military Installations, Economy and People* (Hill Jr. College Press, 1978).

Wright, Bertram C., *The First Cavalry Division in World War II* (1947).

Wright, Marcus J. (Editor), *Texas in the War, 1861-1865* (Hill Jr. College Press, 1965).

Articles

Aston, B. W., "Federal Military Reoccupation of the Texas Southwestern Frontier, 1865-1971," *Texas Military History* (Vol. 8, No. 3), 123-134.

Barnhill, John H., "The Punitive Expedition Against Pancho Villa: The Forced Motorization of the American Army," *Military History of Texas and the Southwest* (Vol. XIV, No. 3), 135-146.

Braddy, Haldeen, "Pershing's Air Arm in Mexico," *Password* (Vol. XII, No. 1), 5-9.

———, "General Scott on Pancho Villa," *Password* (Vol. XIII, No. 2), 8-10.

Brittain, Don L., "A Civilian With Pershing in Mexico," *Password* (Vol. XIV, No. 2), 49-51.

Christian, Garna L., "Adding on Fort Bliss to Black Military Historiography," *West Texas Historical Association Year Book* (Vol. LIV, 1978), 41-54.

de Wetter, Mardee Belding, "Revolutionary El Paso" in three parts *Password* (Vol. III, Nos. 2,3,4).

Goodman, I. B., "Reflections on the El Paso Military Institute," *Password* (Vol. XIV, No. 3), 77-81.

Goldblatt, Kenneth A., "The Defeat of Major I. Lynde, U.S.A.," *Password* (Vol. XV, No. 1), 16-22.

Graham, Stanley S., "Campaign for New Mexico, 1861-1862," *Military History of Texas and the Southwest* (Vol. X, No. 1), 5-28.

Hall, Martin Hardwick, "Negroes With Confederate Troops in West Texas and New Mexico," *Password* (Vol. XIII, No. 1), 11-12.

Howze, Mrs. Robert Lee, "Recollections of Old Fort Bliss," *Password* (Vol. III, No. 1), 30-34.

Jones, Harriot Howze, "My Father—Major General Robert Lee Howze, U.S. Army," *Password* (Vol. XII, No. 3), 67-73.

Jones, Colonel H. Crampton, "The Army Mule," *Password* (Vol. VIII, No. 3), 107-109.

McKinney, Millard G., "The Forgotten Site of Fort Bliss," *Password* (Vol. XXIII, No. 4), 143-148.

McMaster, Richard K., "Vertical Cliffs in Mexico," *Password* (Vol. XXIII, No. 2), 62-64.

——, "Major Jefferson Van Horne," *Password* (Vol. XII, No. 2), 35-42.

——, "A Letter From Major Jefferson Van Horne," *Password* (Vol. XIII, No. 2), 8-10.

——, "The 5th United States Infantry in New Mexico," *Password* (Vol. X, No. 1), 29-32.

——, "Southwestern Military Posts, 1849-1862," *Password* (Vol. IX, No. 1), 35-36.

——, "Records and Reminiscences of Old Fort Bliss," *Password (Vol. VIII, No. 1), 19-32.*

——, *"The Hart's Mill Post, 1880-1893,"Password* (Vol. VIII, No. 4), 131-132.

——, "An Artilleryman in Mexico, 1916," *Password* (Vol. XV, No. 2), 58-71.

——, "Army Town," *Password* (Vol. XI, No. 3), 132-133.

——, "Fort Bliss Diary, 1854-1868," *Password* (Vol. XI, No. 1), 16-25.

——, "Light Artillery at the Pass of the North," *Password* (Vol. II, No. 3), 87-90.

——, "Prince John Magruder at Fort Bliss," *Password* (Vol. III, No. 1), 35-37.

——, "The Ninth Military District: Territory of New Mexico, 1848-1862," *Password* (Vol. V, No. 3), 104-110).

Myers, Lee, "The Fate of Longstreet's Guide," *Password* (Vol. XV, No. 3), 96-101.

Ruhlen, George, "Quitman: The Worst Post At Which I Ever Served," *Password* (Vol. XI, No. 3), 107-126.

——, "Fort Hancock—Last of the Frontier Forts," *Password* (Vol. IV, No. 1), 19-30.

——, "Brazito" (in two parts), *Password* (Vol. 2, Nos. 1 & 2).

——, "The Genesis of New Fort Bliss," *Password* (Vol. XIX, No. 4), 188-217.

Smith, Albion, "Recollections of Camp Cotton," *Password* (Vol. VI, No. 1), 5-23.

Sonnichsen, C. L., "Major McMullen's Invasion of Mexico," *Password* (Vol. 2, No. 2), 38-43.

Starnes, E. C., "War Department Order No. 58: Establish A Post at El Paso...," *El Paso Today* (Nov. 1980), 6-9.

——, "30 Years With 5 Stars," *El Paso Today* (Nov. 1980), 43-44.

Sweeney, Judge Joseph U., "Judge Sweeney Watches A Revolution," *Password* (Vol. XVII, No. 2), 68-73 (edited and annotated by Mildrid Torok).

Warner, Charles P., "Tribute to Fort Bliss," *Suncountry* (Oct. 1973), 8-12.

Wooster, Robert, "Military Strategy in the Southwest, 1848-1860," *Military History of Texas and the Southwest* (Vol. XV, No. 2), 4-16.

"The Taylor Letters: Confederate Correspondence from Fort Bliss, 1861," *Military History of Texas and the Southwest* (Vol. XV, No. 2), 53-60.

Newspapers

The El Paso Times
El Paso-Herald Post
El Paso Lone Star
Fort Bliss Monitor

Unpublished Materials

Air Defense Artillery Museum.

Aultman Collection, El Paso Public Library.

Christian, Garna Loy, "Sword and Plowshare: The Symbiotic Development of Fort Bliss and El Paso, Texas, 1849-1918," *A Dissertation in History*, August, 1977, Texas Tech University.

Connor, Daniel A., "Military Operations in the Southwest, 1861-1865," *Thesis for the Graduate School*, April 1, 1949, Texas College of Mines and Metallurgy.

de Wetter, Mardee, "Revolutionary El Paso, 1910-1917," *Thesis for the Graduate School*, January, 1946, Texas College of Mines and Metallurgy.

Estrada, Richard Medina, "Border Revolution: The Mexican Revolution in the Ciudad Juarez — El Paso Area, 1906-1915," *Thesis for the Graduate Division*, December, 1975, University of Texas at El Paso.

Fort Bliss Replica Museum.

George R. Ruhlen Collection of Fort Bliss materials, Library Archives, University of Texas at El Paso.

Haldeen Braddy Collection of Pancho Villa Materials, Library, University of Texas at El Paso.

Hammons, Nancy Lee, "A History of El Paso County, Texas to 1900," *Thesis for the Graduate School*, September 1942, College of Mines and Metallurgy.

McKinney, Millard G., "Forgotten Flying Field," 1964.

Non-Commissioned Officers Museum.

Post Returns (Partial Collection), Fort Bliss, Library, University of Texas at El Paso.

Public Information Offices at Fort Bliss, White Sands Missile Range and William Beaumont Army Medical Center.

Sandstrum, Allan W., "Fort Bliss: The Frontier Years," *Thesis for the Graduate Division*, June, 1962, Texas Western College.

S.L.A. Marshall Collection of Military History, Library, University of Texas at El Paso.

Tanner, Eric Carroll, "The Texas Border and the Mexican Revolution," Thesis for the Graduate School, August, 1970, Texas Tech University.

Third Armored Cavalry Regimental Museum.

Unfortunately, there is no way to catalog the hundreds of pamphlets and sundry items published by Fort Bliss, William Beaumont Army Medical Center, Biggs Air Force Base and White Sands Missile Range. Some of these materials contained substantial amounts of information, data impossible to list as the publications rarely mentioned authors, editors, publishers, dates, copyrights and page numbers.

Index

ABOUT THE AUTHOR

PEGGY FEINBERG

LEON METZ was born and educated in Parkersburg, West Virginia and has resided in El Paso, Texas since 1952. He is past president of Western Writers of America and was honored by that organization in 1985 with the prestigious Saddleman Award for his overall contributions to interest in western writing. Besides being a prolific writer, he has worked in the West Texas oil fields and law enforcement, as a university archivist, an aide to a large city mayor and as public affairs officer for a bank. Author of twelve books and numerous articles in magazines, newspapers and historical journals, Metz in now a popular television and radio personality and a much sought-after lecturer on gunfighters, military lore, the borderlands and the El Paso, Texas scene.

THE COVER PAINTING

Artist Frederick Carter maintains his studio in El Paso, Texas, has exhibited in many museums throughout the country and is listed in *Who's Who in American Art*. Carter has turned his versatile use of color and light into a special discipline for the assemblage effect used here. Military memorabilia include campaign ribbons, World War I truck, recruiting poster, DH-4 airplane, combat infantryman's badge, artillery and insignia, 1st Cavalry Division shoulder patch, Distinguished Service Cross and Mexican Service Medal.

This Book

was printed by Thomson-Shore, Dexter, Michigan. Type was set by Guynes Printing Company, Complete Printing, RJ Typesetters, and Camille in El Paso, Texas. Text is set in 11 point California. Headings are set in Americana. Text paper is 60-pound Glatfelter.